# McLAIN v. BARBER

---

## Problems and Case File

## THIRD EDITION

Anthony J. Bocchino
Jack E. Feinberg Professor of Litigation
Temple University School of Law

Ronald L. Beal
Professor of Law
Baylor University School of Law

NATIONAL INSTITUTE FOR TRIAL ADVOCACY

**McLain v. Barber**

**Problems and Case File**

Bocchino, Anthony J. and Ronald L. Beal, *McLain v. Barber Problems and Case File*, Third Edition (NITA, 1997).

ISBN 1-55681-540-9
ISBN 13: 978-1-55681-540-9

9/97 9/07

## ACKNOWLEDGMENTS

The authors would like to thank Jeffrey Lenow, M.D., J.D., a 1983 graduate of Temple University School of Law, for his excellent work in preparation of the medical portions of this file relating to Mr. McLain's physical damages. Without Jeff's advice and creativity this file could not have been completed.

In addition, the authors would like to thank Dr. Herbert Horikawa of the Temple University Counseling Center for his assistance in the preparation of the medical portion of this file relating to Mr. McLain's psychological damages.

Finally, the authors express their gratitude to Dean Carl Singley, his administration, and the support staff of the Temple University School of Law for their support in the preparation of this file. Specifically we would like to acknowledge Elaine Willis, Freddie Sanford, Mary Gibson, Ruby Smiley, and Mildred Woodson for their patience and professional assistance in preparing the many drafts of this file.

Anthony J. Bocchino
Ronald L. Beal

# INTRODUCTION

These materials consist of a series of problems and a case file. The problems are divided into ten trial advocacy categories. Each set of problems is preceded by a brief introductory text on the applicable trial advocacy skills and techniques. The case file, *McLain v. Barber*, is a personal injury case arising out of an automobile accident.

The *McLain* case file has been designed to simulate the materials a trial lawyer would have on the eve of trial. The materials have been modified and condensed so that they can be utilized effectively and efficiently within the time restrictions of a trial advocacy program. The *McLain* case file contains the pleadings, the relevant facts, and jury instructions.

All of the problems are based on the *McLain* case file. The problems have been designed to present realistic courtroom situations that regularly confront trial lawyers, which may be utilized to develop and hone trial advocacy skills. In addition to presenting specific trial advocacy issues, these problems provide the participants in the program with an opportunity to become totally immersed in a case that is ready for trial. They provide realistic exercises in sorting, sifting, and weaving together facts and law pertaining to the case, as well as the interrelationships among witnesses and the relationship between the total picture or theme of the case and particular courtroom problems. These problems nurture and develop the technique of trial preparation as well as the particular courtroom techniques that are presented in the problems.

Not all of the problems in these materials will be covered in any single trial advocacy program or course. Indeed, many of the problems within each of the trial advocacy topics are intended as alternatives. Furthermore, depending on a program's length and its purpose, one or more of the trial advocacy topics within these materials may be deleted from a particular trial advocacy program or course.

At the outset we should acknowledge that it is impossible for one person to "teach" another how to become a trial lawyer. Advocacy is an art, the performance of which is dependent on talent and skill mastery. One becomes a trial lawyer through a mixture of predisposition, motivation, observation, doing it, reading how others have done it, and then constantly repeating the latter three—doing, observing, and reading.

It is possible, however, to simulate some of the intellectual, ethical, emotional, and physical demands of trial lawyering in a courtroom-classroom setting. That is what is done in the teaching method developed by the National Institute for Trial Advocacy. These materials are intended to provide a framework for an trial advocacy program based upon the NITA teaching method.

The materials are designed for use in a simulated courtroom session. A judge, whether actual or portrayed, will preside at the front of the courtroom-classroom. A student lawyer will be called upon to begin the problem, e.g., the direct examination in Problem l. The examining student will be opposed by an adversary from among his classmates. The witness will have been prepared and will respond to the examination, as a real witness would in such a courtroom setting.

The student may complete the examination or be interrupted and another student called upon to conclude the examination. The substituting student may pick up where the previous student left off or, with permission of the instructor, may begin again. Generally several students will be called upon to represent both sides before the problem is exhausted and the next problem begun.

Many instructors require universal preparation—each student is prepared to perform at least one side of each problem. Thus, a student may be called upon at any time to undertake an assigned examination.

## McLAIN v. BARBER

## PROBLEMS

## McLAIN v. BARBER
## PROBLEMS

## TABLE OF CONTENTS

*Page*

# INTRODUCTION

The following problems are based on the *McLain v. Barber* case file, and they are intended to simulate realistic courtroom situations. Advance preparation is essential to their successful utilization as instructional materials. The materials within the *McLain* case file must, of course, be mastered before attempting to perform the problems in a courtroom setting.

All years in these materials are stated in the following form:

> YR-0 indicates the actual year in which you are trying the case (i.e., the present year);
> YR-1 indicates the next preceding year (please use the actual year);
> YR-2 indicates the second preceding year (please use the actual year); etc.

## DIRECT, CROSS, AND REDIRECT EXAMINATION

The ability to examine and oppose the examination of witnesses in open court in an adversary setting is the most basic skill of the trial lawyer. Yet, the most common criticism is that they are unable to conduct proper, intelligent, and purposeful examinations and to oppose these examinations.

As with any skill, practice is the only sure way to achievement. The practice should be conducted with some guidelines in mind.

1. The purpose of any witness examination is to elicit information.

2. The basic format is an interrogative dialogue.

3. The witness is probably insecure. She is appearing in a strange environment and is expected to perform under strange rules. This is a handicap you must overcome on direct and an advantage you have (and may choose to exploit) on cross.

4. Your questions should be short, simple, and understandable to the witness, the judge, and the jury on both direct and cross-examination.

    (a) It is imperative that your audience—the judge and the jury—understand your question so that they reasonably can anticipate and comprehend the answer.

    (b) On direct examination the insecurity or anxieties of the witness will be increased if he does not understand your questions.

    (c) On cross-examination the complex argumentative question provides a refuge for the witness to evade the point.

5. As a general proposition, you may not lead on direct except as to preliminary matters or to refresh the recollection of the witness. Both of these exceptions are discretionary with the judge.

6. In any event, on direct examination leading questions and the perfunctory answers they elicit are not persuasive.

7. On cross-examination you may lead and you should do so. Control of the witness on cross is imperative.

8. At the outset of direct examination, have the witness introduce herself. Then, place her in the controversy on trial, and elicit the who, where, when, what, how, and why of the relevant information the witness has to offer. Then quit. Do not be repetitious.

9. If you know that the cross-examination will elicit unfavorable information, consider the possible advantage of eliciting it during your direct examination.

10. Do not conduct a cross-examination that does nothing other than afford the witness an opportunity to repeat his direct testimony.

    (a) If there is nothing to be gained by cross-examination, waive it.

    (b) If you can accomplish something by cross-examination, get to it. Organize your points and make them.

    (c) Be cautious about cross-examining on testimony elicited on direct that was favorable to your position. You may lose it.

    (d) Be cautious about asking questions to which you do not know or cannot reasonably anticipate the answer. Be particularly cautious in these situations if the only evidence on the point will be the unknown answer.

11. Listen to (do not assume) the answers of the witness. As an examiner, you are entitled to responsive answers. Insist on them by a gentle repetitive question on direct or a motion to strike on cross. Of course, if the answer is favorable, accept it and return to the pending question.

12. Objections to the form of the question must be made before an answer is given. If the question reveals that the answer sought will be inadmissible, an objection must precede the answer. The grounds of the objection should be succinctly and specifically stated. If the question does not reveal the potential inadmissibility of the answer, but the answer is inadmissible, a prompt motion to strike should be succinctly and specifically stated. Only the interrogator is entitled to move to strike an answer on the sole ground that it was unresponsive to the question. If the answer is unresponsive and contains objectionable matter, then the opposing counsel is entitled to object.

13. If an objection to the content of the answer (e.g., relevancy, hearsay, etc.) as opposed to the form of the question, is sustained, then the interrogator should consider the need for an offer of proof at the first available opportunity. If an objection to the form of the question is sustained, then the interrogator should rephrase the question to cure the objection.

## PROBLEM 1
## Dennis McLain

Assume that the case is at trial and the plaintiffs' first witness is Dennis McLain.

(a) For the plaintiffs, conduct a direct examination of Mr. McLain limited to the issue of liability.

(b) For the defendants, conduct a cross-examination of Mr. McLain limited to the issue of liability.

(c) For the plaintiffs, conduct any necessary redirect examination.

## PROBLEM 2
## Alexander Barber

Assume that the case is at trial and the plaintiffs have presented their case in chief. Assume further that the defendants' motion for nonsuit has been denied. The defendants call as their first witness Alexander Barber.

(a) For the defendants, conduct a direct examination of Mr. Barber.

(b) For the plaintiffs, conduct a cross-examination of Mr. Barber.

(c) For the defendants, conduct any necessary redirect examination.

## PROBLEM 3
## Mark Dennison

Assume that the case is at trial and the plaintiffs have called Dennis McLain. The plaintiffs' next witness is Mark Dennison.

(a) For the plaintiffs, conduct a direct examination of Mr. Dennison.

(b) For the defendants, conduct a cross-examination of Mr. Dennison.

(c) For the plaintiffs, conduct any necessary redirect examination.

## PROBLEM 4
## Steven Petersen

Assume that the case is at trial and the defendants have called Alexander Barber. The defendants' next witness is Steven Petersen.

(a) For the defendants, conduct a direct examination of Mr. Petersen.

(b) For the plaintiffs, conduct a cross-examination of Mr. Petersen.

(c) For the defendants, conduct any necessary redirect examination.

## PROBLEM 5
## Jeremy Brown

Assume that the case is at trial and the defendants have called Alexander Barber and Steven Petersen. The defendants' next witness is Jeremy Brown.

(a) For the defendants, conduct a direct examination of Mr. Brown.

(b) For the plaintiffs, conduct a cross-examination of Mr. Brown.

(c) For the defendants, conduct any necessary redirect examination.

## HANDLING AND INTRODUCTION OF EXHIBITS

The ability to examine and oppose the examination of witnesses in open court in an adversary setting is the *most* basic skill of the trial lawyer.

The second basic skill of the trial lawyer is the proper, efficient, and orderly handling and introduction of tangible evidence. Again, however, a common criticism of the trial bar is its lack of facility in this truly simple undertaking.

This is all the more regrettable when one considers the highly persuasive quality of relevant exhibits. Jurors (and judges, too) trust them. They are the real thing. They don't exaggerate as witnesses do, and they don't overstep their bounds as lawyers do. Many a case has been won or lost because a particularly intriguing exhibit was received in evidence or was excluded.

The four touchstones for the handling and introduction of exhibits are:

(l) authenticity,

(2) relevance,

(3) the hearsay rule, and

(4) the best evidence rule.

These four touchstones must be satisfied before an exhibit can be received in evidence. Some call it "laying the foundation." By whatever phrase, the essential element is testimony establishing that the exhibit is authentic and relevant and complies with both the hearsay and best evidence rules.

Authenticity is simply a demonstration that the exhibit is what it purports to be. Is this thing—whatever it is—that is being offered in evidence, *prima facie* that which it purports to be?[*] The essential requirement is testimonial vouching for the thing unless, of course, authenticity is established by admissions in the pleadings, discovery, or a request to admit. See, for example, Federal Rule of Civil Procedure 36.

Relevance, as well as the hearsay and best evidence rules, is intrinsically dependent on the issues raised in the case and the purpose for which the exhibit is offered in evidence. In each instance, however, the foundation demonstrating that the exhibit is relevant and that it complies with the hearsay and best evidence rules must be laid.

For each exhibit, counsel should check the four touchstones and then lay the foundation necessary for its admission in evidence through the testimony of one or more witnesses. As in the case of witness examination, the skill of handling and introducing exhibits is developed by practice and is conducted with certain guidelines in mind.

---

* The standard is a *prima facie* showing of authenticity, as the court determines admissibility. The weight to be assigned to the particular piece of evidence is left to the factfinder.

1. Select with care the witness or witnesses you will use to lay the foundation for your exhibits. A mistake here could be fatal.

2. Because the introduction of exhibits usually is done through witnesses, keep in mind the basic principles of witness examination.

3. Have the exhibit marked for identification by the appropriate court official (usually the court reporter or clerk) at the earliest opportunity. Many lawyers have their exhibits marked for identification prior to trial in the sequence in which they expect to use them. Some judges insist on this. It is a good practice in cases involving many exhibits. But also consider the advantages to be gained from a brief pause for the witness and a little bit of the lawyer doing his "thing" that attends your stepping to the bench and requesting in a voice the jury can hear, "Your Honor, may the reporter mark this document (or object) defendant's Exhibit 1 for identification?"

4. Once the exhibit has been marked for identification, include that identification in any reference you make to the exhibit and see to it that your opponent, the witnesses, and the judge do likewise. Never permit the record to read merely, "this letter" or "that bottle" or "the photograph," etc.

5. Proceed to "lay the foundation" as follows:

    (a) Elicit from the authenticating witness those facts that qualify him or her to authenticate the exhibit. For example, have the witness say he saw the gun in the robber's hand.

    (b) Have the witness identify the exhibit by saying, for example, that State's Exhibit 1 is the gun (or looks like the gun) the witness saw in the robber's hand.

    (c) If the condition of the exhibit is a factor in its relevancy, either elicit testimony that its condition has not changed between the event and the time of trial or offer a testimonial explanation of the change in condition.

    (d) If the exhibit is a reproduction of a place, a thing, or an event (e.g., a photograph or a tape recording), elicit testimony that it fairly and accurately portrays that which it purports to portray.

    (e) If more than one witness is required to authenticate or connect the exhibit, withhold your offer until you have completed your foundation. A premature offer and rejection can condition a judge to reject the exhibit later when the foundation has been completed.

6. Once the foundation for an exhibit has been laid properly, offer it in evidence and obtain a ruling on its admissibility. In some jurisdictions an exhibit may not be offered during cross-examination, and in those instances the formal offer of the exhibit is reserved to your case in chief or rebuttal.

7. When you are opposing the introduction of an exhibit, you are entitled to conduct a cross-examination on the foundation before the court rules on the offer. The scope of this cross-examination, often referred to as a *voir dire* on the exhibit, is limited to the admissibility of the exhibit. The proponent of the exhibit should be alert so to limit the *voir dire* on the exhibit and not permit the opponent to conduct a general cross-examination on the weight that is to be given to the exhibit.

8. When you are opposing the introduction of exhibits, be on the alert for changed conditions and distortions (particularly in photographs). Insist that an adequate testimonial explanation of the changes be given by the authenticating witness.

9. Do not permit your opponent to display tangible items in the presence of the jury until they are marked for identification and proffered to the witness for identification.

10. Keep a separate record of the status of your exhibits and those of your opponent. Know at all times their identification numbers, their general descriptions, the witness or witnesses who authenticated them, and whether they have been offered and received or excluded. Many lawyers keep a columnar record somewhat like this:

Plaintiff's Exhibits

| No. | Description | Witness | Date or Page of record offered | Date or Page of record received | Date or Page of record refused |
|---|---|---|---|---|---|
| 1. | Letter from Jones | Smith | 6/1/YR-1 p. 138 | 6/1/YR-1 p. 140 | |
| 2. | Hammer | Jones | 6/2/YR-1 p. 200 | | 6/2/YR-1 p. 210 |

11. At the close of your case, if you are uncertain as to the status of any of your exhibits, reoffer them before you rest.

Each exhibit has its own standards of authenticity and admissibility. For our purposes, they are better demonstrated than described.

(1) Photographic Material.

## PROBLEM 6
## X-Rays

Assume that the case is at trial.

Part 1

Assume that the x-rays cannot be introduced as part of the hospital records.

(a) For the plaintiffs, introduce into evidence the x-rays. You may use any witness or witnesses you desire to lay the foundation for the exhibits. Examine the witness or witnesses to the extent necessary to lay the foundation and then offer the exhibits. Be prepared to discuss your choice of witness(es).

(b) For the defendants, oppose the examination of the witness(es) and the offer of the exhibits. Be prepared to *voir dire* the witness(es) on the admissibility of the exhibits.

Part 2

(a) For the plaintiffs, introduce into evidence the x-rays as part of the hospital records. You may use any witness or witnesses you desire to lay the foundation for the exhibits. Examine the witness or witnesses to the extent necessary to lay the foundation and then offer the exhibits. Be prepared to discuss your choice of witness(es).

(b) For the defendants, oppose the examination of the witness(es) and the offer of the exhibits. Be prepared to *voir dire* the witness(es) on the admissibility of the exhibits.

(2) Writings.

## PROBLEM 7
## Police Report

Assume that the case is at trial.

(a) For the plaintiffs, introduce into evidence the police report of Officer Dominic Fusco. You may use any witness or witnesses you desire to lay the foundation for the exhibit. Examine the witness or witnesses to the extent necessary to lay the foundation and then offer the exhibit. Be prepared to discuss your choice of witness(es).

(b) For the defendants, oppose the examination of the witness(es) and the offer of the exhibit. Be prepared to *voir dire* the witness(es) on the admissibility of the exhibit.

## PROBLEM 8
## Weather Report

Assume that the case is at trial.

(a) For the plaintiffs, introduce into evidence the weather report for February 11, YR-1. You may use any witness or witnesses you desire to lay the foundation for the exhibit. Examine the witness or witnesses to the extent necessary to lay the foundation and then offer the exhibit. Be prepared to discuss your choice of witness(es).

(b) For the defendants, oppose the examination of the witness(es) and the offer of the exhibit. Be prepared to *voir dire* the witness(es) on the admissibility of the exhibit.

## PROBLEM 9
## Invoice

Assume that the case is at trial.

(a) For the defendants, introduce into evidence the invoice from Dan Rosen Cadillac relating to the Barbers' YR-1 Cadillac. You may use any witness or witnesses you desire to lay the foundation for the exhibit. Examine the witness or witnesses to the extent necessary to lay the foundation and then offer the exhibit. Be prepared to discuss your choice of witness(es).

(b) For the plaintiffs, oppose the examination of the witness(es) and the offer of the exhibit. Be prepared to *voir dire* the witness(es) on the admissibility of the exhibit.

## PROBLEM 10
## Invoice

Assume that the case is at trial.

(a) For the plaintiffs, introduce into evidence the invoice from Kirsch Chevrolet/Mazda relating to the McLains' YR-2 Toyota. You may use any witness or witnesses you desire to lay the foundation for the exhibit. Examine the witness or witnesses to the extent necessary to lay the foundation and then offer the exhibit. Be prepared to discuss your choice of witness(es).

(b) For the defendants, oppose the examination of the witness(es) and the offer of the exhibit. Be prepared to *voir dire* the witness(es) on the admissibility of the exhibit.

## PROBLEM 11
## Emergency Room Record

Assume that the case is at trial.

(a) For the defendants, introduce into evidence the Nita City Memorial Hospital Emergency Room Record of February 11, YR-1, relating to Dennis McLain. You may use any witness or witnesses you desire to lay the foundation for the exhibit. Examine the witness or witnesses to the extent necessary to lay the foundation and then offer the exhibit. Be prepared to discuss your choice of witness(es).

(b) For the defendants, oppose the examination of the witness(es) and the offer of the exhibit. Be prepared to *voir dire* the witness(es) on the admissibility of the exhibit.

## PROBLEM 12
## Medical Bill

Assume that the case is at trial.

(a) For the plaintiffs, introduce into evidence the medical bill for Dennis McLain that was submitted by Dr. Vitali. You may use any witness or witnesses you desire to lay the foundation for the exhibit. Examine the witness or witnesses to the extent necessary to lay the foundation and then offer the exhibit. Be prepared to discuss your choice of witness(es).

(b) For the defendants, oppose the examination of the witness(es) and the offer of the exhibit. Be prepared to *voir dire* the witness(es) on the admissibility of the exhibit.

## PROBLEM 13
## Medical Records

Assume that the case is at trial.

(a) For the defendants, introduce into evidence the medical records of the Lenow Institute of Outpatient Myopathic Rehabilitation. You may use any witness or witnesses you desire to lay the foundation for the exhibit. Examine the witness or witnesses to the extent necessary to lay the foundation and then offer the exhibit. Be prepared to discuss your choice of witness(es).

(b) For the plaintiffs, oppose the examination of the witness(es) and the offer of the exhibit. Be prepared to *voir dire* the witness(es) on the admissibility of the exhibit.

## PROBLEMS IN THE USE OF DEMONSTRATIVE OR VISUAL AIDS

1. **Demonstrative or Visual Aids in General.** In addition to exhibits that are offered and received in evidence on the basis of their intrinsic relevance to the case, demonstrative or visual aids frequently are used by lawyers during examinations of witnesses. These aids are exhibits that assist witnesses in explaining their testimony. Such exhibits, in and of themselves, are not relevant to the case; their relevance flows from the fact that by assisting a witness in testifying, they enhance the probative value of the testimony. The phrase "demonstrative *aid*" as opposed to "demonstrative *evidence*" indicates that the exhibit's evidentiary value is derived from its role in assisting the witness as opposed to any intrinsic evidentiary value.

The foundation for demonstrative or visual aids is based on the same four touchstones that govern other exhibits: authenticity, relevance, the hearsay rule, and the best evidence rule. For authenticity and the hearsay and best evidence rules, the foundation depends on the particular exhibit and will be determined on an individual basis. The general analysis of the necessary foundation, however, is the same as that used for all other exhibits.

The relevance foundation for demonstrative or visual aids is testimony establishing that the exhibit will assist a witness in explaining his or her testimony. By permitting the court or the jury to more fully understand the value of the testimony of a witness, the exhibit enhances the probative value of the testimony. The countervailing arguments on the question of relevance are that the exhibit raises collateral issues, wastes time, or is unduly prejudicial. In ruling on the use of demonstrative or visual aids, courts employ the classic relevancy balancing test, meaning the use of such aids is discretionary with the court. Most judges are inclined to permit their use as aids to understanding witness testimony if they will not unduly emphasize that testimony.

2. **Diagrams.** In many jurisdictions, diagrams are *sui generis* and may be classified as either demonstrative evidence or demonstrative aids depending on their relevance to the case. If testimony establishes that a diagram is a fair and accurate representation of something that is relevant, then the diagram is demonstrative evidence. The foundation required for diagrams is essentially the same as that required for photographs. (What is the purpose of the offer? Is the exhibit, when used for that purpose, relevant? Does the exhibit fairly and accurately represent what it purports to represent?) If what is depicted by an authentic diagram is not itself relevant to the case, the diagram is not admissible as demonstrative evidence. But if the diagram is authentic and will assist a witness in explaining his testimony, then it is helpful to a better understanding of the evidence and relevant. The diagram is then admissible as a demonstrative or visual aid for use in assisting the witness. In summary, a diagram usually is admissible as demonstrative evidence if it is authentic and in itself relevant to the case, and a diagram is admissible as a demonstrative or visual aid if it is authentic and will assist a witness in testifying.

In some jurisdictions, however, diagrams are not admissible as demonstrative evidence under any circumstances and may be used in court solely as demonstrative or visual aids. Although a diagram may be authentic (i.e., it is what it purports to be), courts in those jurisdictions do not consider a diagram to be a sufficiently fair and accurate representation of the real thing to permit its admission as demonstrative evidence. Those courts' rationale is that a diagram by nature only depicts a one-dimensional view. Those courts do permit diagrams to be used to assist witnesses in testifying. In other words, they allow diagrams to be used as demonstrative or visual aids but not as demonstrative evidence.

In all jurisdictions, a diagram need not be drawn to scale to be admitted or used at trial. The fact that a diagram is not to scale affects its weight and not its admissibility or use. If the diagram is not being offered or represented as a scale drawing, then the factfinder can consider and weigh that factor in evaluating the exhibit.

3. **Problems in the Use of Demonstrative or Visual Aids**. Problems in the use of demonstrative or visual aids generally occur because of the lawyer's lack of skill in dealing with the device once she has been granted permission from the court to use it. One common shortcoming is the lawyer's failure to introduce the witness to the aid prior to the time she testifies. It is not sufficient that the witness be familiar with the subject matter illustrated in the aid. Unless the witness has seen the device and has become sufficiently familiar with the particular illustration involved, the testimony can be disastrous.

The trial lawyers also should be careful to preserve the record for appeal. Words such as "right here" and "at this point" will have no meaning to an appellate court. If the witness's testimony is to have any value on appeal, it must be translated in some manner into words or markings.

## PROBLEM 14
## Diagram

Assume that the case is at trial. For the purposes of this problem, assume that Officer Dominic Fusco is the first witness for the plaintiffs.

(a) For the plaintiffs, conduct a direct examination of Officer Fusco using the diagram attached to his deposition in the case file. Prepare a diagram large enough to be seen by the jury.

(b) For the defendants, oppose the use of the diagram and conduct a cross-examination of Officer Fusco.

(c) For the plaintiffs, conduct any necessary redirect examination.

## IMPEACHMENT AND REHABILITATION OF WITNESSES

1. Impeachment.

Although it is a part of the cross-examiner's art, impeachment is a sufficiently difficult problem in itself to warrant separate consideration.

(a) The cross-examiner must consider not only how to impeach, but also whether the witness should be impeached at all. Just as the trial lawyer should not cross-examine in some situations, he often may decide wisely that, although impeaching evidence is available, it should not be used. If the witness has not hurt your case, usually it is better not to impeach and risk offending the jury. If the testimony of a witness can be turned to your advantage, as in the case of a truly impartial expert witness, do so and do not impeach.

(b) Foundation for impeachment by prior inconsistent statement:

(1) Under the law of most jurisdictions, the witness must be confronted with a prior inconsistent statement during cross-examination. If his or her attention has not been called to the earlier statement, extrinsic evidence of it will not be admissible. Cross-examination should be specific as to the time, circumstances, and content of the earlier statement.

(2) The rule requiring a foundation for prior inconsistent statements is relaxed under the Federal Rules of Evidence. Federal Rule 613(b) provides that the witness must be "afforded an opportunity to explain or deny" the prior inconsistent statement in order for extrinsic evidence to be admissible, but no time sequence is specified. Therefore, as long as the witness is available to explain the inconsistency if he so desires, extrinsic proof is admissible.

(3) Most advocates will prefer to lay a foundation on cross-examination regardless of whether or not it is required under the rules. The reason for this is twofold. First, the witness may admit the statement, making extrinsic evidence unnecessary. More significant, confronting a witness with her own inconsistency often will have a dramatic impact that cannot be duplicated by introducing evidence of the earlier statement through another person.

(c) If the witness denies making an earlier statement, be prepared to prove it by extrinsic evidence.

(d) If the witness admits making an inconsistent or otherwise impeaching statement, do not ask questions that give him an opportunity to explain it away, unless you are certain that this cannot be done. The attorney who has called the witness will have an opportunity on redirect examination to elicit explanations, if any are available. This affords you the opportunity for recross.

(e) There is no need, and it is usually harmful, to dwell on the impeaching matter after it has been brought out in cross-examination. Remember, you have a closing argument.

2. Rehabilitation.

If a witness has been impeached during cross-examination, counsel must evaluate whether to attempt to rehabilitate the witness on redirect examination.

(a) As with any redirect examination, counsel should limit the scope of the redirect to those items in which the witness needs an opportunity to explain or amplify upon his testimony after the cross-examination. Redirect examination and rehabilitation of a witness is not the time to rehash the direct testimony once again.

(b) In considering whether to rehabilitate a witness on redirect examination, counsel should first of all be absolutely certain that the witness has, in fact, been impeached. If the witness has not been effectively impeached, do not attempt to rehabilitate the witness as you may only worsen matters.

(c) Rehabilitation generally consists of providing the witness with an opportunity to explain the circumstances pertaining to the impeachment and to elicit any "exculpatory" factors. Give the witness the opportunity to put the impeachment in context.

(d) If the impeachment can be explained, do it; if not, leave it alone on redirect as you just may worsen matters.

(e) If the witness has been impeached by a prior inconsistent statement, counsel should consider the admissibility of any prior consistent statements. See 801(d)(1)(B) of the Federal Rules of Evidence. Prior consistent statements are generally admissible if they rebut an express or implied charge of recent fabrication.

## PROBLEM 15
## Alexander Barber

Assume that during direct examination Mr. Barber testified that directly before the accident that he was traveling at a safe rate of speed and further that he considers himself a safe driver.

(a) For the plaintiffs, conduct the cross-examination of Mr. Barber limited to the issues raised by his testimony above.

(b) For the defendants, conduct any necessary redirect examination.

## PROBLEM 16
## Dennis McLain

Assume that during direct examination Mr. McLain testified that he performed all rehabilitative exercises and followed all of the prescribed treatment concerning his wrist injury.

(a) For the defendants, conduct the cross-examination of Mr. McLain limited to the issues raised by his testimony above.

(b) For the plaintiffs, conduct any necessary redirect examination.

## DISCOVERY DEPOSITIONS

No factor has had a greater impact on the trial of lawsuits in the last forty years than the increased availability of discovery devices for learning about an opponent's case. In a civil case, if these devices are used properly, virtually nothing in your opponent's case should surprise you. Increasingly, this also is becoming true in criminal cases.

Following are a few words about what is perhaps the most important discovery device, the deposition:

1. In a deposition taken for purposes of discovery, the object is not to establish your own case or to impeach the witness. Rather, the goals are to obtain information for your use and to pin the witness down to a story for possible impeachment at trial.

2. Unlike cross-examination, there usually is no need to cut the witness off if he gives a rambling answer. Let the witness tell his story; volunteered information may be useful.

3. Make sure, however, that the witness has stated his version of the events with sufficient certainty that the statements can be used for impeachment at trial. Once you are sure that the witness has made a firm and usable statement, leave the matter alone and go on to the next point.

4. Pursue all leads; don't avoid areas that are sensitive for your case. You will need to know what the witness will say, even though it hurts you.

5. If you are representing a deponent, or if the witness is friendly to your side of the case, ordinarily you should cross-examine only when clarification of testimony might avoid or lessen the impact of some anticipated impeachment. Usually you will not cross-examine at all.

6. Remember, however, that in most jurisdictions a deposition may be read if the deponent is unavailable. Therefore, you should object to questions that are improper in form. You need not object to questions that ask for inadmissible evidence in order to prevent the use of that evidence at the trial.

7. If the question invades some area of privilege or violates another rule of evidence, and you do not want the witness to answer the question, you may advise your client that she need not respond. Counsel examining the witness should press for another answer until the witness has indicated that she will not answer. A court ruling on the propriety of the question can be obtained later.

## PROBLEM 17
## Dennis McLain

(a) For the defendants, conduct the discovery deposition of Dennis McLain.

(b) For the plaintiffs, represent Mr. McLain.

## PROBLEM 18
## Jennifer McLain

(a) For the defendants, conduct the discovery deposition of Jennifer McLain.

(b) For the plaintiffs, represent Ms. McLain.

## PROBLEM 19
## Alexander Barber

(a) For the plaintiffs, conduct the discovery deposition of Alexander Barber.

(b) For the defendants, represent Mr. Barber.

## PROBLEM 20
## Dr. Michael Gratch

(a) For the defendants, conduct the discovery deposition of Dr. Michael Gratch.

(b) For the plaintiffs, represent the McLains at this deposition.

## PROBLEM 21
## Dr. Rachel Kaplan

(a) For the plaintiffs, conduct the discovery deposition of Dr. Rachel Kaplan.

(b) For the defendants, represent the Barbers at this deposition.

# ADVANCED DIRECT AND CROSS-EXAMINATION

<u>Proving Damages</u>

Some of the most important and difficult issues in the examination of witnesses in civil cases concern damages. The following problems are intended to raise some of those issues.

## PROBLEM 22
## Dennis McLain

(a) For the plaintiffs, conduct the direct examination of Mr. McLain on the issue of damages.

(b) For the defendants, conduct a cross-examination of Mr. McLain on the issue of damages.

(c) For the plaintiffs, conduct any necessary redirect examination.

## PROBLEM 23
## Jennifer McLain

(a) For the plaintiffs, conduct a direct examination of Ms. McLain on the issue of damages.

(b) For the defendants, conduct a cross-examination of Ms. McLain on the issue of damages.

(c) For the plaintiffs, conduct any necessary redirect examination.

## EXAMINATION OF SKILLED OR EXPERT WITNESSES

As a conservative estimate, eighty percent of all trials in courts of general jurisdiction involve the examination of skilled or expert witnesses. For example, in personal injury cases there are medical experts and experts in accident reconstruction; in criminal cases there are chemical, ballistics, fingerprint, and handwriting experts; and in commercial cases there are economists and market analysts. The opportunities for use of skilled or expert witnesses are limited only by human knowledge and the trial lawyer's ingenuity. Accordingly, no lawyer is worthy of the name "trial lawyer" until she has mastered the techniques that attend the direct and cross-examination of skilled or expert witnesses.

The function of the expert witness is to bring to the trial of a case knowledge beyond the everyday and to apply that knowledge to the facts in the case so that jurors may better determine the issues.

The basic guidelines are stated simply, but they are not so simple to apply.

1. **Qualifications**. The proposed expert witness must be qualified by training or experience in a recognized field of knowledge that is beyond that of the average layman.*

2. **Explanation of Expertise**. If the field of knowledge is at all esoteric, the expert witness should provide a brief explanation of it, particularly with reference to its application to the case at hand.

3. **Ruling on Qualifications as an Expert**. In some jurisdictions after the witness's qualifications have been elicited, the witness is tendered to the court as an expert in his or her field, and the court either accepts or rejects the witness as an expert at that time. Some courts, however, are reluctant to give their imprimatur to the witness's testimony or to rule on the witness's qualifications as an expert prior to hearing the actual opinion the expert will be asked to give. In those jurisdictions, the direct examination simply proceeds unless there is an objection, at which time the court rules.

4. **Cross-Examination on Qualifications**. The opposing counsel may *voir dire* (cross-examine) the witness on his or her qualifications at the time the witness is tendered to the court as an expert witness or, if that procedure is not utilized, before the witness is permitted to express her opinion.

---

* Under the Federal Rules of Evidence, the test is whether the witness's knowledge, training, or experience will *assist* the trier of fact in understanding the evidence or determining a fact in issue. Note also that the witness, if qualified as an expert, may testify in the form of an opinion *or otherwise*. Fed.R.Evid. 702.

5. **Basis of Opinion**. The direct examination should elicit a description of what the expert did with regard to the case and the facts that are the basis of the opinion.*

The facts that may be used as the basis for the expert's opinion and may be elicited on direct examination are limited to those facts that:

(a) the expert personally observed,

(b) were elicited in the courtroom and heard by the expert, or

(c) were transmitted to him hypothetically.

In the federal courts and some state courts, facts that were made known to the expert outside of court and other than by his or her own perception also may be used if they are of a type reasonably relied upon by experts in the expert's field. See Fed.R.Evid. 703.

In most state courts, the hearsay rule and the other traditional principles of admissibility apply to expert testimony. Opposing counsel should keep an ear carefully tuned for the application of these principles during the expert's direct examination. In the federal courts and some state courts that have relaxed the hearsay rule and the other traditional requirements for admissibility for expert testimony, the expert may testify to, and base his opinion on, facts that are not admissible in evidence.

6. **Opinion**. The expert's opinion may not be speculation or conjecture. Rather, it must be an opinion to a reasonable degree of certainty within the expert's field. Most courts require that the opinion be elicited in a two-question sequence: (l) Do you have an opinion as to ______?, and then (2) What is that opinion? This gives opposing counsel an opportunity to object before the opinion is heard by the jury.

When the expert's opinion is based on facts that the expert did not personally observe or hear in the courtroom, the hypothetical-question format is required in most state courts. However, in the federal courts and some state courts, the hypothetical question no longer is required, and the trial lawyer has the option of using it or not. Fed.R.Evid. 703, 705. When this format is optional, the trial lawyer's decision is a matter of trial strategy, which depends on many factors. Perhaps some of those factors will be demonstrated in the exercises.

---

* In most state courts the direct examination *must* elicit the factual basis for the expert's opinion as a foundation prerequisite for the expert stating his opinion. This is the method for ensuring that the expert's opinion is based on admissible evidence.

While, in the federal courts, the underlying facts for the expert's opinion need not be disclosed on direct examination, the expert will be required to disclose them on cross-examination. Fed.R.Evid. 705. The court, however, has the discretion to require that the underlying facts be disclosed prior to the expert stating his opinion if the interest of justice so requires. *See also* Fed.R.Evid. 703.

The underlying facts for the expert's opinion are usually quite persuasive, and most trial lawyers will make them an integral part of their direct examination. The trial lawyer has the option in federal court, and she may tailor the direct examination to meet the needs of the particular case.

The primary objections that are available to opposing counsel when the hypothetical-question format is utilized are:

(a) that the hypothetical question included facts not in evidence, or

(b) that it did not include relevant facts that are in evidence.

Thus, in a complicated case the hypothetical question can be quite cumbersome. In anything but the most routine case it can be a delicate procedure with pitfalls to snare the unwary.

7. **Cross-Examination**. The expert witness may be cross-examined with respect to his or her opinion on the basis of:

(a) the expert's qualifications,*

(b) other facts in the case, or

(c) the published opinions of other recognized authorities in the field (learned treatises).

---

* The cross-examination on qualifications, discussed in paragraph 4, is a *voir dire* on the admissibility of the expert's opinion. The cross-examination here goes to the weight of the expert's opinion. Counsel should weigh carefully whether to cross-examine in both instances or to elect one or the other.

## PROBLEM 24
## Dr. Michael Gratch

Assume that all the witnesses for the plaintiffs have testified except Dr. Vitali.

(a) For the plaintiffs, conduct the direct examination of Dr. Gratch.

(b) For the defendants, conduct the cross-examination of Dr. Gratch.

(c) For the plaintiffs, conduct any necessary redirect examination.

## PROBLEM 25
## Dr. Jean Vitali

Assume that Dr. Vitali is the last witness for the plaintiffs.

(a) For the plaintiffs, conduct the direct examination of Dr. Vitali.

(b) For the defendants, conduct the cross-examination of Dr. Vitali.

(c) For the plaintiffs, conduct any necessary redirect examination.

## PROBLEM 26
## Dr. Rachel Kaplan

Assume that Dr. Kaplan is the last witness for the defendants.

(a) For the defendants, conduct the direct examination of Dr. Kaplan.

(b) For the plaintiffs, conduct the cross-examination of Dr. Kaplan.

(c) For the defendants, conduct any necessary redirect examination.

## JURY SELECTION

If one were to select ten able trial lawyers at random and ask them how to select a jury, one would get ten different answers. The answers would range from, "Take the first twelve (or six) and put them in the box," to "Examine each juror firmly and searchingly." Both extremes have pros and cons. Similarly, so do the more moderate methods.

There is virtual unanimity among trial lawyers that the makeup of the jury is important. There is also agreement among those who watch trial lawyers at work that we do a pretty fair job of jury selection, regardless of how we do it or why we excuse those who are excused.

There are certain basic guidelines that should be followed in selecting a jury.

1. In those jurisdictions that permit the lawyers to interrogate the veniremen, realize that this is your first direct contact with the jurors. Don't alienate them. Don't try them.

2. Know the statutory qualifications for jurors and the case-law grounds for challenge for cause.

3. Know the number of peremptories to which you are entitled.

4. Never challenge a juror for cause in the presence of that juror unless you have a peremptory by which you can excuse him if your challenge is overruled.

5. Use your peremptories wisely. Do not spend them too quickly.

6. Be alert for jurors whose background and experience indicate that they possess knowledge particularly relevant to the facts in the case. You may end up with a one-juror jury.

7. Be alert for jurors whose background and experience indicate a high potential of prejudgment of the case adverse to your position. They may hang the jury.

8. Seek a cross-section of the community, but bear in mind that studies have indicated a correlation between ethnic-socio-economic background and juror vote.

## PROBLEM 27
## Voir Dire

For the plaintiffs, conduct the *voir dire* of the jury panel. Be prepared to indicate which jurors you would attempt to strike for cause and which jurors on whom you would use a peremptory challenge.

For the defendants, conduct the *voir dire* of the jury panel. Be prepared to indicate which jurors you would attempt to strike for cause and which jurors on whom you would utilize a peremptory challenge.

Jury Information Sheet

Please assume the role of a person whom you know well so that you will be able to answer *voir dire* questions in that role. Please be realistic. Try to pick a role that likely would be represented on jury panels and *not a role of an eccentric.* By taking the role of an eccentric, you would impair the realism and benefit of the exercise for your fellow students, both those who serve as counsel and those who observe the exercise.

Please fill in the following form and be prepared to use it at the session on Problem 30. You may be asked to deliver it to the instructor during the session.

Your real name: ______________________________

Information About You in Your Assumed Role

1. Name: ______________________________

2. Age: ______________________________

3. Address in Nita City: ______________________________

   Characterize your neighborhood: ______________________________

4. Length of residence in Nita City: ______________________________

5. Occupation: ______________________________ Duties in that occupation:

   ______________________________

6. Marital status: ______________________________

7. Ages of children: ______________________________

8. Number of years of education: ______________________________

9. Other relevant information: ______________________________

   ______________________________

## OPENING STATEMENT

The opening statement is akin to the first scene in a play—it had better capture the audience. It is the trial lawyer's first direct contact with the jury, save in those jurisdictions that permit substantial lawyer participation in the *voir dire* examination of the jury. Even in those states, in the overwhelming majority of cases it is the lawyer's first opportunity to present the jury with an intelligent, cohesive description of the case.

Some trial lawyers tend to minimize the importance of an opening statement. We do not. We regard it as crucial to the successful outcome of the trial.

There is no excuse for a poor opening statement. The opening statement is essentially *ex parte*; it can and should be prepared well in advance of its presentation, and it should be rehearsed.

It is a skill that can be mastered with practice more readily than any other skill. The general guidelines for opening statements are:

1. Practice, rehearse, try out, and listen to your opening statement before you make it. Have a wife, a husband, a friend, or a colleague listen. As you rehearse, you can listen too. Preferably, have a lay audience.

2. Recognize the opening statement for what it is: a prologue or synopsis of a play, a blueprint, a travel guide folder, or the old favorite—the picture on the jigsaw puzzle box. We do not urge that you use these similes when you address the jury. We do urge that you recognize the opening statement for what it is. Indeed, in conjunction with the evidentiary portion of the trial and the closing argument, it is the trial lawyer's application of the oldest of public speaking techniques: tell your audience what you are going to say, say it, and tell them what you have said.

3. Recognize the opening statement for what it is not: it is not an argument. This is not the time to infer, plead, or fulminate. It is a time to tell the jury what the case is about and what you expect your evidence will be.

4. An opening statement in behalf of the plaintiff or prosecution should include:

    (a) A request of the court and the jury: "If the court please, ladies and gentlemen of the jury."

    (b) An introduction of yourself, your client, your opponent, and his client, if not already done sufficiently during jury selection.

    (c) A cohesive, succinct, and confident summary of what your evidence will be.

    (d) A conclusion, indicating that at the close of the case you will return and request the jury to find in favor of your client.

(e) Some lawyers include the following either at the beginning or the end of the opening statement:

(1) A brief statement of the nature of the case.

(2) A brief statement of the issues of the case.

(3) A candid acknowledgment that the burden of persuasion rests on you and the degree of the burden.

(4) A reading of the indictment or information (which is required in some jurisdictions).

5. An opening statement in behalf of the plaintiff or prosecution should not include:

(a) Reference to evidence the availability or admissibility of which is doubtful.

(b) Anticipated defenses or defense evidence.

6. In most cases, an opening statement for a defendant should be made immediately following the plaintiff's or prosecution's. If the court has granted you permission to defer your opening statement until the close of your opponent's case, be certain the jury knows this. Be very cautious about waiving a defendant's opening statement entirely.

7. An opening statement in behalf of a defendant should include:

(a) A request of the court and the jury: "If the court please, ladies and gentlemen of the jury."

(b) An introduction (or reintroduction) of yourself and your client, if not already done sufficiently during jury selection.

(c) An admonition that opening statements are not evidence.

(d) An acceptance of the issues as defined by your opponent plus any additional ones that will be raised by the defense.

(e) A reinforcement of the principle that the burden of persuasion rests with your opponent, plus a candid recognition of any issues in respect to which the burden rests with you.

(f) A cohesive, succinct, and confident (but nonargumentative) reference to anticipated deficiencies in your opponent's evidence plus a like summary of what your evidence will be.

(g) A conclusion indicating that at the close of the case you will return and request the jury to find in favor of your client.

8. As with your counterpart, a defense counsel's opening statement should not include references to evidence the availability or admissibility of which is doubtful.

## PROBLEM 28
## Opening Statement

(a) For the plaintiffs, deliver the opening statement.

(b) For the defendants, deliver the opening statement.

## CLOSING ARGUMENT

Here is the advocate in his final and finest hour! "She won it with her closing argument! She was magnificent!" Legion are the legends of summations. Really, however, a lawsuit is won during the trial, not at the conclusion of it. It is won by the witnesses and the exhibits and the manner in which the lawyer paces, spaces, and handles them.

The likelihood of a lawyer snatching victory from the jaws of defeat with his or her closing argument is so slight as to hardly consideration. (*Compare*, last of the ninth game-winning home runs; *but see,* Bobby Thompson's shot heard 'round the world in *Giants v. Dodgers* (1951).)

On the other hand, lawsuits are lost by fumbling, stumbling, incoherent, exaggerated, vindictive closing arguments.

This is not intended to minimize the importance of the closing argument. It is merely to relegate it to its proper position, which is a summation of the evidence that has preceded it and a relation of that evidence to the issues in the case.

Although the closing argument is not as controllable as the opening statement, it is very close to it, close enough that we can say that there is no excuse for a poor closing argument.

Many trial lawyers begin to prepare their closing arguments with their first contact with the case: as the facts make their initial impression on their minds. That is when they are as close to being jurors as they ever will be. From that first impression forward they shape and reshape their closing arguments as the facts develop. Finally, they shape the trial to what they believe their strongest arguments will be; they prove their arguments.

Thus, the closing argument has a considerable impact on the trial because an able trial lawyer knows that an argument without evidence to support it is no argument at all.

The basic guidelines for closing arguments are:

1. Think about, prepare, and rehearse your closing argument before trial, leaving sufficient flexibility to meet the exigencies of trial.

2. Think about, modify, and rehearse your closing argument at each break in the trial in light of the record to date.

3. Think about, modify, and, if time permits, rehearse your closing argument at the close of the evidence and the conference on instructions.

4. Base your closing argument on the issues, the evidence, the burden of proof in the case, and your client's right to a verdict.

5. From the standpoint of format:

   (a) Address the court, the jury, and your opponent.

   (b) Tell the jury your purpose–to summarize the facts and relate them to the issues in the case.

   (c) Make your argument.

   (d) Tell the jury what its verdict should be.

   (e) Sit down.

6. From the standpoint of delivery: do not shout, do not engage in personalities, and do not tell the jury what you believe. Act and speak as though you do believe, to the depths of your soul, every word you are uttering. If you can't do this, don't argue.

7. As for some of the canned approaches:

   (a) Do not repeat in chronological order the testimony of each witness. Give the jury some credit; it has heard the witnesses. Put it all together.

   (b) Do not tell the jury what you say is not evidence. Why belittle your argument? The judge will do that for you.

   (c) Do not assume a burden of persuasion that is not yours.

## PROBLEM 29
## Closing Argument

(a) For the plaintiffs, deliver the first closing argument.

(b) For the defendants, deliver the closing argument.

(c) For the plaintiffs, deliver any rebuttal argument.

# McLain v. Barber

---

# CASE FILE

**McLAIN v. BARBER**
**CASE FILE**

## TABLE OF CONTENTS

*Page*

## STATEMENT OF THE CASE

*McLain v. Barber* is a personal injury action arising out of an automobile accident. The accident took place on February 11, YR-2, at about 1:30 p.m. at the intersection of the Vine Street entrance ramp and U.S. 76 East in Nita City. At the time of the accident it was snowing. The plaintiff was driving a YR-3 Toyota. The defendant was driving a YR-2 Cadillac which belonged to his wife.

The accident occurred as the plaintiff attempted to enter onto U.S. 76 East from the Vine Street entrance ramp. The defendant was driving east on U.S. 76.

The plaintiff contends that the defendant was driving too fast for conditions and as a result the defendant lost control of his car and rear-ended the plaintiff. The plaintiff's car was pushed into a retaining wall and the plaintiff, Dennis McLain, suffered a broken wrist and substantial injuries to his back. Mr. McLain, who was a potter before the accident, has sued for the value of his car, which was destroyed, medical expenses, loss of income, and pain and suffering. His wife, Jennifer McLain, has sued for loss of consortium.

The defendants contend that Alexander Barber was driving at an appropriate speed for conditions and that the accident was the result of Mr. McLain swerving into Mr. Barber's lane of traffic. The defendants have counterclaimed for the damages to their car. Mr. Barber was not injured in the accident.

The case is designed so that the issue of liability and damages can be easily bifurcated.

For the purposes of this file, assume the following geographical facts. Nita City is located in the center of the state of Nita. Williamstown, Nita, is located in the far southeastern corner of the state of Nita. Scottsville, Nita, is located in the far northeastern corner of the state of Nita.

The available witnesses are as follows:

Plaintiff:
- Dennis McLain
- Jennifer McLain
- Officer Dominic Fusco
- Mark Dennison
- Dr. Michael Gratch
- Dr. Jean Vitali

Defendant:
- Alexander Barber
- Jeremy Brown
- Steven Petersen
- Dr. Rachel Kaplan

All years in these materials are stated in the following form:

YR-0 indicates the actual year in which you are trying the case (i.e., the present year);
YR-1 indicates the next preceding year (please use the actual year);
YR-2 indicates the second preceding year (please use the actual year); etc.

IN THE CIRCUIT COURT OF
DARROW COUNTY, NITA
CIVIL DIVISION

| | | |
|---|---|---|
| DENNIS McLAIN and JENNIFER McLAIN,<br><br>Plaintiffs,<br><br>v.<br><br>ALEXANDER BARBER and LYNN BARBER,<br><br>Defendants. | ) | CIVIL ACTION<br>CA79-0073-R |

COMPLAINT

Dennis McLain and Jennifer McLain, individually, for their causes of action against the defendants, state and allege as follows:

I

Jurisdiction of this action is conferred upon this Court by 28 N.S.A. § 1332.

II

That the matter in controversy exceeds, exclusive of interests and costs, the sum of Fifty Thousand and no/100 ($50,000) Dollars.

III

That the plaintiffs, Dennis McLain and Jennifer McLain, at all times material herein were citizens of the State of Nita.

IV

That at all times material herein, the defendants, Alexander Barber and Lynn Barber, were citizens of the State of Nita.

V

That at all times material herein the plaintiff, Dennis McLain, was the owner and operator of a YR-3 Toyota.

VI

That on February 11, YR-2, the defendant, Lynn Barber, was the owner of a YR-2 Cadillac Seville automobile.

VII

That on February 11, YR-2, the defendant, Alexander Barber, was the operator of the YR-2 Cadillac Seville automobile with the implied and/or express permission and consent of the owner-defendant, Lynn Barber.

VIII

That on February 11, YR-2, at or near the entrance ramp of the Vine Street Expressway West entering onto U.S. Highway 76 East, in the City of Nita, Darrow County, and State of Nita, the defendant, Alexander Barber, as the duly authorized agent of the defendant, Lynn Barber, so negligently and carelessly drove and operated the YR-2 Cadillac Seville automobile as to cause said automobile to collide with and against a YR-3 Toyota owned and operated by the plaintiff, Dennis McLain.

IX

That as a direct and proximate result of the negligent and careless conduct of the defendant, Alexander Barber, as the duly authorized agent of the defendant, Lynn Barber, the plaintiff, Dennis McLain, was caused to suffer severe, permanent, and disabling injuries, great bodily human harm, and mental pain and suffering all to his detriment in the amount of Two Hundred and Fifty Thousand and no/100 ($250,000) Dollars.

X

That as a direct and proximate result of the negligent conduct of the defendants as stated above, the plaintiff, Dennis McLain, has been prevented and will continue to be prevented from engaging in the conduct of his profession and livelihood with the subsequent loss of income, profits, reputation, and professional awards all to his detriment in the amount of One Million and no/100 ($1,000,000) Dollars.

XI

That as a direct and proximate result of the negligent conduct of the defendants as stated above, the plaintiff, Dennis McLain, has sustained the total loss and use of his YR-3 Toyota all to his detriment in the amount of Nine Thousand and no/100 ($9,000) Dollars.

XII

That as a direct and proximate result of the negligent conduct of the defendants as stated above, the plaintiff, Jennifer McLain, has sustained the loss of consortium, of the aid and comfort and enjoyment of her husband-plaintiff, Dennis McLain, all to her detriment in the amount of Three Hundred Thousand and no/100 ($300,000) Dollars.

WHEREFORE, The plaintiffs, Dennis McLain and Jennifer McLain, demand judgment against the defendants, Alexander Barber and Lynn Barber, jointly and severally, in the amount of One Million Five Hundred Fifty-Seven and no/100 ($1,557,000) Dollars, together with costs and disbursements herein and such other relief to which said plaintiffs are entitled in law or in equity.

Respectfully Submitted,

Diane Restler
Attorney at Law

IN THE CIRCUIT COURT OF
DARROW COUNTY, NITA
CIVIL DIVISION

| | | |
|---|---|---|
| DENNIS McLAIN and JENNIFER McLAIN, Plaintiffs, | ) | |
| v. | ) | CIVIL ACTION CA79-0073-R |
| ALEXANDER BARBER and LYNN BARBER, Defendants. | ) | |

JOINT ANSWER

Alexander Barber and Lynn Barber, for their answer to the plaintiffs' complaint, state and allege as follows:

I

Deny each and every matter and thing, subject or allegation except as hereinafter admitted or answered by a qualified response.

II

Admit the allegations set forth in paragraphs IV, VI, and VII of the plaintiffs' complaint.

III

That as to the allegations set forth in paragraphs I, II, III, V, IX, X, XI, and XII of the plaintiffs' complaint these answering defendants have insufficient information to form a belief as to the truth of those allegations and demand strict proof thereof.

IV

As to the allegations in paragraph VIII of plaintiffs' complaint, admit that on February 11, YR-2, at or near the entrance ramp of the Vine Street Expressway West entering onto U.S. Highway 76 East, the City of Nita, Darrow County, in the State of Nita, the defendant, Alexander Barber, was involved in an automobile accident with the plaintiff, Dennis McLain, but specifically denies that the accident was caused by any negligent or careless conduct on the part of either defendant, Alexander Barber or Lynn Barber.

V

AFFIRMATIVE DEFENSE

That for an Affirmative Defense, on February 11, YR-2, the plaintiff, Dennis McLain, over whom this answering defendant had no control, was so negligent and careless in the operation of his YR-3 Toyota automobile, that as a direct result of his conduct, an accident occurred.

VI

That this court lacks jurisdiction over the subject matter set forth in the plaintiffs' complaint.

VII

That the plaintiffs fail to state a cause of action upon which relief can be granted.

VIII

That this court lacks jurisdiction over the person of these answering defendants.

COUNTERCLAIM

The Defendant, Lynn Barber, for her cause of action against the plaintiff, Dennis McLain, states and alleges as follows:

IX

Realleges the allegations set forth in paragraphs I through VIII herein.

X

That on February 11, YR-2, at or near the entrance ramp of the Vine Street Expressway West entering onto U.S. Highway 76 East, in the City of Nita, Darrow County, and State of Nita, the plaintiff, Dennis McLain, so negligently and carelessly drove and operated his YR-3 Toyota so as to cause said automobile to collide with and against the YR-2 Cadillac Seville owned by the defendant, Lynn Barber.

XI

That as a direct and proximate result of the negligent and careless conduct of the plaintiff, Dennis McLain, the defendant Lynn Barber's YR-2 Cadillac Seville sustained physical damage resulting in fair and reasonable repair costs of Two Thousand, Five Hundred and no/100 ($2,500) Dollars.

WHEREFORE, the defendants, Alexander Barber and Lynn Barber, demand judgment against the plaintiffs, Dennis McLain and Jennifer McLain, as follows:

1. As to the ANSWER, these answering defendants demand judgment of dismissal with prejudice of the plaintiffs' pretended causes of action, together with costs and disbursements herein;

2. As to the COUNTERCLAIM against the plaintiff, Dennis McLain, the defendant, Lynn Barber, demands judgment in the amount of Two Thousand, Five Hundred and no/100 ($2,500) Dollars together with costs and disbursements herein and such other relief to which said defendants are entitled in law or in equity.

Respectfully submitted,

Ronald L. Benton

Ronald L. Benton
for Defendants Barber

IN THE CIRCUIT COURT OF
DARROW COUNTY, NITA
CIVIL DIVISION

| | | |
|---|---|---|
| DENNIS McLAIN and JENNIFER McLAIN,<br><br>Plaintiffs,<br><br>v.<br><br>ALEXANDER BARBER and LYNN BARBER,<br><br>Defendants. | ) | CIVIL ACTION<br>CA79-0073-R |

ANSWER TO COUNTERCLAIM

Dennis McLain, plaintiff for his answer to the counterclaim of the defendant, Lynn Barber, states and alleges as follows:

I

Denies each and every matter and thing, subject or allegation except as hereinafter admitted or answered by a qualified response.

II

Denies the allegations set forth in paragraphs IX, X, and XI of the defendant's counterclaim and demands strict proof thereof.

WHEREFORE, the plaintiff, Dennis McLain, demands judgment of dismissal with prejudice of the defendant, Lynn Barber's pretended counterclaim, together with costs and disbursements herein.

Respectfully submitted,

____________________________

Diane Restler
Attorney at Law

## DEPOSITION OF DENNIS McLAIN*

My name is Dennis McLain. I live at 1414 Winding Way in Williamstown, Nita. I am 31 years old, married, and have one child. My wife's name is Jennifer and my daughter, who is six years old, is named Lauren. She was born on December 17, YR-7. My wife and I met while we were both undergraduate students at Williamstown University. My wife was a business major, and I majored in fine arts. We graduated in YR-9.

I was born in Scottsville, Nita. My parents moved to Williamstown in YR-18 for my father's job. He is retired now, and they have moved back to Scottsville. My wife was born in Williamstown, Nita. Both her parents are dead.

In July, YR-8, I was arrested for possession with intent to distribute marijuana. I had been a marijuana user while in college. In YR-8, my wife and I were living on a farm outside of Williamstown. I was growing marijuana near the back of our property for our own use. I pleaded guilty to the charge and served three months in the county jail. I have not had any other trouble with the law either before that or since. I do not use marijuana or any other drug, including alcohol, at the present time or for the past seven years, with the exception of an occasional glass of wine, since my daughter was born.

While I was in college I became interested in pottery. My wife and I are in the pottery business in Williamstown. We own a shop, "The Potter's Place," where we sell the work of a number of potters. The shop formerly sold a good deal of my pottery, but since the accident I have been unable to produce the quality of work I once had, so the sale of my work is a very small part of our income since I broke my wrist and injured my back. Actually my wife owns the shop in her name, and I worked for the shop. I worked on the artistic side; my wife is in charge of the business. We started the business in YR-7 and have had steady growth up until the accident when I broke my wrist. You'll have to talk to my wife about the business end of the business, but I know that in the year before the accident we earned about $90,000 between us. Jennifer's income from the shop was about $55,000-$60,000. My income after materials and equipment, before I was injured, was about $35,000. My income from the shop now is only about $15,000 as my money making from the pottery business is limited to the teaching I do. Jennifer's income has also dropped some because she no longer has my pottery to sell. Although she's

---

* The transcript of McLain's deposition was excerpted so that only his answers are reprinted here. Assume that this is a true and accurate rendering of those answers.

taken on some additional artists, her income for last year was down to approximately $45,000, so our family income has dropped to about $60,000 for last year.

One of the ways that I got my name around in the pottery business was to show my work at various shows in and around the state of Nita. In recent years, Jennifer has also used the shows to find new talent whose work we could sell out of our shop.

One of the shows that we've been going to for the past six years is the Nita Crafts Show which runs for two weeks every February, at the Civic Center in Nita City. The Nita Crafts Show is juried and exhibitors appear by invitation, and it is considered to be the most important of the year in the state of Nita. In YR-3 I was named as best in show for potters in my category. I was in Nita City for that show when the accident happened.

On February 6, YR-2, I left Williamstown and drove to Scottsville to see my parents. On February 11, YR-2, I drove to Nita City and checked into the Darrow Plaza Hotel which is located just off Vine Street and between 16th and 17th Streets. I actually checked in at about 11:00 a.m. on Friday. My wife didn't come to my parents' house with me because Lauren was sick. Also, our car, a YR-3 Toyota Lift Back, was packed up with all the pottery for the show. The plan was for Jennifer and Lauren to take the train to Nita City Friday and stay there for the two weeks of the show, and then we'd drive back together.

I don't know if you remember, but that Friday was the day of the big snow storm. I was a little worried because the snow hit Williamstown pretty bad. Also Lauren, although a lot better, was still a little under the weather.

After I checked into the hotel, I called Amtrak and found out that the train from Williamstown was late but due in at 1:30 p.m. The snow was really coming down and the wind was swirling, but there wasn't a large accumulation at that time. At about 12:45 p.m. I got in my car to drive over to 30th Street station to pick up Jennifer and Lauren. This was the first year we'd stayed at the Darrow Plaza, but I looked at a map and it appeared that I could get to the train station by going west on Vine Street to U.S. 76 Eastbound and get right off at the train station. The car was packed with my pottery. The plan was to pick up Jennifer and Lauren and then go to the Civic Center and set up our booth. I drove north on 16th Street and took a left on Vine Street and followed the signs to 76 East. The roads were slippery and the visibility poor, but because I had front wheel drive I made the turn off of Vine

Street onto the entrance of 76 East. The entrance merged into traffic on the left side of Route 76 East.

As I got to the end of the entrance ramp and pulled out onto 76 East, I realized that I couldn't get off at the train station so I intended to go up one exit and come back around to the train station. As I entered the highway it looked like the road was clear. I couldn't use the rear view mirror because the pottery blocked my view, but I could see out of the right side windows and use the right side-view mirror. As I pulled into the highway, my wheels spun, then caught and I swerved a little to my right. I'm sure I never went into the right lane. It was at that point that I caught a glimpse of a large car (that I now know to be Mr. Barber's Cadillac) bearing down on me very quickly. The driver (Barber) seemed to lose control and swerve into my lane. The left front of his car clipped my right rear and drove me into the wall.

I guess I sensed the impact because I braced myself on the steering wheel. When I hit the wall, the air bag inflated, and I heard a snap and felt an incredible pain in my right wrist. I knew then that it was broken, and I remember thinking, "God, what's going to happen to my career?" The next thing I knew a guy was helping me out of my car. I now know that his name is Mark Dennison. He took me back to his car and called on his car phone for the police and a tow truck. My car was eventually towed to his shop (he was a mechanic). The car was a total (see McLain Deposition Exhibit 1) and all but a few pieces of pottery were broken. Because he was so nice, I gave Dennison what was left of the pottery and we also sent him and his wife a complete set of mugs. A policeman showed up within a few minutes, and he later took me to the emergency room at Nita Memorial Hospital. (I've marked the diagram to show how and where the accident happened.) (See McLain Deposition Exhibit 2.)

My wrist really hurt, and my back was also a little stiff, but I was more concerned about my wife and kid. While I waited for what seemed forever but was actually only about an hour, I made a call to the train station and they somehow got over to the hospital. They got there sometime after I finally got in to see the doctor. The doctor seemed to be in a real hurry, I guess because there were a lot of people in the emergency room. I told her about both my wrist and that my back was stiffening up, but she was distracted at best. Because of the doctors's apparent disinterest and the confusion at the hospital, I insisted that my wrist be treated by my own doctor. That seemed to upset the emergency room doctor, but she gave me some pain medication and we got back to the hotel by cab.

As I said, you'll have to talk to Jennifer about the money, but I knew we lost the money we paid for our booth—$1,000. (See McLain Deposition Exhibit 3.) Also, most of the pottery was destroyed in the accident. It was worth about $6,500 retail. I expected to sell virtually all of it at the crafts show as that had been our experience the year before.

I've also been very depressed because I can't do the work that I love. I've been seeing a psychiatrist, Dr. Vitali, for the past four months. That has cost me $250/weekly (two visits per week) for a total of $4,250. (See McLain Deposition Exhibit 4.) I don't know how long that expense will continue. My doctor in Williamstown is Michael Gratch. I've been seeing him as my physician since right after my parents moved to Williamstown about eighteen years ago. I think I first saw him for a broken arm, my left. He also treated me for a broken leg that occurred after a tennis match. Both of these broken bones occurred while I was in high school. I take medication for asthma which I'm told makes me more susceptible to broken bones. Dr. Gratch also treated me for a back problem I had in YR-6 when I hurt myself lifting a fairly large box of pottery.

Dr. Gratch treated me for the broken wrist and the back problems that have developed from the accident. In addition I was treated at the Lenow Institute of Outpatient Therapy for my wrist. My therapist was Linda Rosen. I have some difficulty with her—a personality conflict. She didn't seem very sympathetic concerning my injury, but I guess that's because she does this kind of work all the time. As you can imagine, I was very depressed about not being able to do my work. I did follow the exercise routine, however, and I'm told that my wrist has healed as much as it's going to be. I did miss a few appointments, but that was because of car trouble or something like that. Even though I didn't like Ms. Rosen, I did do everything I was told with one exception. I am an avid softball player and did play once over Labor Day weekend, YR-2. I was a little sore but got over it very quickly. Rosen made a big deal over the whole thing, but I think that's because she didn't like me.

My back has also given me a lot of trouble. Since I became a potter for a living, I have had some minor problems with my back, from all the hours sitting at the wheel, as well as from the lifting of the pottery. I also had one more serious problem in YR-6 when my back popped when I was lifting a box of pottery. That injury resolved after about a month of heat and massage therapy. At first I wasn't concerned with my back, although I did mention it to the emergency room doctor, assuming that it would resolve itself. But when it wasn't any better by two weeks after the accident, I went to Dr. Gratch to see if he could help. My back has gotten progressively worse so that it bothers me all the time and the pain radiates down my left leg and sometimes into my right thigh. My back prevents me from any vigorous physical activity. Dr. Gratch has told me that surgery might be a treatment option some time in the future, but I'd like to avoid it if I could. I'd rather put up with the pain than risk surgery, especially because there are no guarantees that surgery will fix the problem I have. I take ibuprofen on a fairly regular basis, and when it really acts up I take a prescribed muscle relaxant called robaxin. I have also received some heat and massage treatment at the Williamstown Back Rehabilitation Center, approximately 15 sessions since I was injured, and that helps some, but the threat of pain is always there, even when I'm pain free for short periods of time.

The bottom line is that I have to realize that my career as a potter is over. My wrist will never allow me to perform the fine motor skills necessary for the kind of art-pottery that I used to be able to create and even if my wrist was OK, my back injury would make it difficult to do the close work for extended periods of time that the kind of pottery work I used to do required. I'm trying to deal with this and Dr. Vitali has been helpful, but I'm afraid my mental state has taken a lot out of both Jennifer and Lauren. I've been very depressed and moody, and not much fun to be around. Jennifer and I have not been as close as we always were, either emotionally or sexually. And Lauren seems to be afraid to upset me, which is hard on a little kid. As I said, I'm trying to work through this, but it's not easy, especially with the nagging reminder of my back problems. It's hard to be optimistic when you're in pain.

I have looked at the bill for booth rental at the Nita City Crafts Show and the medical bills you've shown me and they are accurate. (See McLain Deposition Exhibits that follow this deposition.)

I've read this deposition and it is accurate.

(After the deposition was transcribed, it was signed by the deponent, Dennis McLain.)

Certified by:

Ann E. Hall

ANN E. HALL
Certified Shorthand Reporter

February 14, YR-2

Invoice No: 258

Kirsch Chevrolet/Mazda

West Nita, Nita

| Item | Work Completed | Parts | Labor | Total |
|---|---|---|---|---|
| | | | | |
| | | | | |
| | Cracked frame and | | | |
| | extensive damage to | | | |
| | entire car — YR-3 | | | |
| | Toyota Liftback | | | |
| | TOTALED | | | |
| | | | | |
| | | | | |
| | Blue Book Value - $5,800.00 | | | |
| | | | | |
| | Salvage 985.25 | | | |
| | Towing + Appraisal 198.55 | | | |
| | 786.70 | | | |
| | | Sub-total | | |
| | Pay to Insurance | TAX | | |
| | Company for D. McClain | TOTAL | | |
| | $786.70 | | | |
| | Mark Dennison | | | |

***NITA CRAFTS SHOW***
***The Civic Center***
***Nita City, Nita***

February 12-27, YR-2

| | |
|---|---|
| Received from: | The Potter's Place, Williamstown, Nita<br>Jennifer McLain |
| Amount: | $1,000 |
| For: | Booth Rental |

Edward Smith

Edward Smith, Director

McLain Deposition Exhibit 4

**Jean Vitali, M.D.**
**Practice Limited to Psychiatry**
**410 Medical Arts Building**
**Williamstown, Nita**

Patient: Dennis McLain

Insurance: Blue Cross/Blue Shield

| | | |
|---|---|---|
| Services Rendered: | 33 sessions @ $125.00 = | $4,125 |
| | Report Preparation File | 250 |
| | Total Due | $4,375.00 |

McLain Deposition Exhibit 5

# NITA CITY MEMORIAL HOSPITAL
# DEPARTMENT OF EMERGENCY SERVICES

---

| | |
|---|---|
| Patient: | Dennis McLain<br>1414 Winding Way<br>Williamstown, Nita |
| Insurance: | B/C - B/S |
| Date: | 2/11/YR-2 |
| Amount Due: | $450.00 |

Harold Wolfram

Harold Wolfram
Records Custodian

McLain Deposition Exhibit 6

## Michael A. Gratch, M.D.

25 Lendough Avenue
Williamstown, Nita
732-7200

| | |
|---|---|
| Patient: | Dennis McLain |
| Address: | 1414 Winding Way<br>Williamstown, Nita |
| Treatment Provided: | Treatment for Colles fracture of the right arm |
| Amount Due: | $5,780.00 |

McLain Deposition Exhibit 7

# LENOW INSTITUTE OF OUTPATIENT MYOPATHIC REHABILITATION

Hospital of the Williamstown University

| | |
|---|---|
| Patient: | Dennis McLain<br>1414 Winding Way<br>Williamstown, Nita |
| Physician: | Michael A. Gratch, M.D. |
| Insurance: | Blue Cross/Blue Shield |
| Fee for Services Rendered: | $5,285.00 |

McLain Deposition Exhibit 8

# WILLIAMSTOWN BACK REHABILITATION CENTER

**Medical Arts Building**
**1495 Chestnut Street**
**Williamstown, NI**

Patient: Dennis McLain

Insurance: BC/BS

Referring Physician: Dr. Gratch

Bill for services rendered: 2/YR-2 - 4/YR-2

15 heat and massage session @ $150

Total due: $2,250

## DEPOSITION OF JENNIFER McLAIN*

My name is Jennifer McLain. I live at 1414 Winding Way in Williamstown, Nita. I am thirty years old and married to Dennis McLain. We have one child, Lauren, who is seven years old. She was born on December 17, YR-7. I met my husband while we were both undergraduate students at Williamstown University. I was a business major. Dennis majored in fine arts. We graduated in YR-9 and were married that summer on July 31.

I was born and raised in Williamstown. My parents are both dead. Dennis was born and raised in Scottsville, Nita, and moved to Williamstown when he was a teenager. His parents are now retired and living in Scottsville.

After Dennis and I got married we lived in Williamstown on a farm just outside of town. We were both marijuana users in college, and Dennis was growing some marijuana on our property. He got caught and pleaded guilty to the charge. The judge wanted to teach him a lesson so he sent him to jail for three months. That was in YR-8. He was released in November, YR-8. Neither of us have used any drugs since I got pregnant with Lauren in YR-7. We might have a glass of wine when we go out to dinner, but that's all.

Dennis and I are in the pottery business. Actually he has the talent and I run the business. He became interested in pottery while in college and is actually quite good. He's won a number of awards for his work. About six years ago we opened up a retail shop in Williamstown called "The Potter's Place." In the beginning Dennis was the sole potter, but as time went on we started to sell the work of other people as well. At the time of the accident we had a working relationship with seven potters including Dennis. Since the accident, because Dennis can't work, we've signed up three other potters. I work on a one-third commission on all the pottery I sell.

Actually, the business is in my name alone. Dennis is an artist and didn't want to get involved in marketing. Because I was a business major I'm very interested in that sort of thing. I do all the work including keeping the books. The business has grown steadily and in the year before the accident, YR-3, we grossed about $173,000. The gross reflects the amount I take in from the sale of pottery and from the classes that Dennis used to teach. Dennis was paid by the business for his pottery just like the other artists as well as being paid for his classes. In YR-3 the profits from the business were about $60,000, so

* The transcript of Jennifer McLain's deposition was excerpted so that only her answers are reprinted here. Assume that this is a true and accurate rendering of those answers.

with Dennis's income of about $35,000 we made pretty good money. (Assume that the plaintiffs produced their tax records and they verify the figures given by both Dennis and Jennifer McLain.)

Dennis's income from the sale of his pottery and classes in YR-3 was approximately $47,000 before the cost of equipment and materials. I think he netted about $35,000 in YR-3. His net income for the previous years was $28,000 in YR-4, $21,500 in YR-5, and $16,200 in YR-6.

One of the ways we marketed Dennis's work was to go to shows throughout Nita and the surrounding states. In addition, since I opened the business, I have gone to the shows to sign up other potters to sell their work in my shop. We have always taken Lauren with us to the shows and made them into family occasions. At the shows you rent a booth, set it up, and sell out of the booth.

In February of YR-2 we were scheduled to go to the Nita Crafts Show which is held every year at the Nita Civic Center in Nita City. It is the most important juried show of the year, and potters can show their work by invitation only. In YR-3 Dennis's work was recognized as best in the show for pottery. We had planned to drive up to Scottsville to see Dennis's parents for a few days and then go on to the show in Nita City. We had reservations for the two weeks to stay at the Darrow Plaza Hotel. As it turned out Lauren got sick so she and I stayed in Williamstown and did not make the trip to Scottsville. Dennis went ahead, and the plan was for Lauren and me to take the train up to Nita City and meet Dennis. Even though there was a bad snow storm, the trains were running and Lauren and I left home at about 7:00 a.m. on Friday, February 11, YR-2.

The train was a little late and arrived in Nita City at about 1:45 p.m. Dennis wasn't at the train station, but I was paged when the train got in. I was told that Dennis had been in an accident and was at the Nita City Memorial Hospital Emergency Room. We took a cab there and waited around for Dennis. The emergency room was a madhouse, I guess because the storm caused a lot of accidents. Dennis got out of the examination room and his right wrist was all wrapped up. He said that he wanted to get back to Williamstown to get it fixed up by our own doctor, Dr. Gratch. He also said that his back, that had given him some trouble from time to time before the accident, was stiffening up.

Because of the storm we weren't able to get back to Williamstown until the next Monday. We took the train because our car had to be fixed. It ended up being a total loss that our insurance paid for. Apparently, most of the pottery was broken in the accident. It was worth about $6,500 - $7,000 retail. We were confident that we could sell most or all of it because that had been our experience the last few years.

Even though the emergency room doctor gave Dennis some pain medication, he was in a lot of pain while we were in Nita City. Not only was his wrist hurting him, but his back was also an increasing problem. I tried to get him to go back to a doctor in Nita City, but he refused. In addition to the pain he was very worried about the effect of his wrist injury on his career.

Once we got back to Williamstown, Dennis saw the doctor and his broken wrist was put in a cast. Dennis had to go to a rehab center for both his wrist and his back. For his back he received some heat and massage therapy that seemed to help somewhat, but he has experienced a good deal of pain in his back and down his left leg. Dennis had hurt his back once before in YR-6 or YR-7, but that problem seemed to go away after about a month. His back keeps him from sitting or standing in one place for any extended period of time, which makes working as a potter very difficult. I know that Dr. Gratch has mentioned that surgery might be an option for Dennis sometime in the future, but Dennis is opposed to surgery.

The therapy for Dennis's wrist injury was more involved and required a good deal of physical therapy. Even though he didn't care for his therapist, Ms. Rosen, he did do all of his exercises, but they made him depressed because of the pain and the progress wasn't very quick. It doesn't look like it will ever be 100%, and even though he's tried to work he just can't do it. He hangs around the shop a lot but is real depressed. He's been seeing a psychologist and that seems to help, but he's still real depressed.

As I said, I've signed up three new potters, but their work didn't and doesn't sell like Dennis's. Our profits from the business for the year since the accident were down to approximately $45,000. I had expected that the gross sales on Dennis's work would have been at least $35-40,000 for this year, but because we lost all that pottery in Nita City and Dennis can't work, it has really gone down to zero. The three new potters just aren't as good as Dennis, and it is unlikely that together they can match Dennis's profitability. With the loss of Dennis's sales for the business, we will certainly have a down year when, with the addition of the new potters, our business and its profitability should have grown. We would have signed up the potters even without Dennis's injury so the loss to the business both from his work and his classes amounts to a net loss of $13,000 to $15,000. In addition, Dennis's personal income from the sale of his pottery is down to near zero, so his sole income is from the lessons he teaches at the rate of about $15,000 per year.

It is not easy to talk about, but Dennis's injury has presented some difficulties in our relationship. Up until the time of the accident our relationship was a good and strong one. Part of the strength came from the fact that we had an equal partnership in the business. He was the artist and I was the business person. Since his art has been taken away from him, he is a different person. Our relationship has been strained, and although we still love each other there is a tension that just was never there before. We seem to argue about little things that never mattered before. I know that Dennis doesn't see the change, but with everything that's happened to him I can't really expect too much. The tension has even affected our sex life. It is not as good as before. But the main problem is his moodiness and the effect it has on my state of mind as well as Lauren's.

I have read the above transcription of my deposition and it is accurate.

(After the deposition was transcribed, it was signed by the deponent, Jennifer McLain.)

Certified by:

Ann E. Hall

ANN E. HALL
Certified Shorthand Reporter

## DEPOSITION OF MARK DENNISON*

My name is Mark Dennison. I am 31 years old and live at 940 Christian Street in Nita City. I grew up in the Oak Lane neighborhood of the city and attended public schools and graduated from high school in YR-14. I am married with two daughters, Lauren and Susan. My wife is from South Nita City and we live in her old neighborhood around the corner from her parents. I work as a mechanic and as an assistant manager for foreign car repairs at Kirsch Chevrolet/Mazda in West Nita, Nita. I have been working there for the past eleven years after I got out of the Army. I served for three years; one year in West Germany and two years at Fort Dix in New Jersey. I was assigned to the motor pool while I was in the service and received an Honorable Discharge.

I don't remember anything unusual during the week before the accident. I know I was at work all week because the manager was gone and I was in charge. Business was pretty hectic, but not unusual for that time of year. On Thursday night before the accident my wife and I had a few friends over for supper. I think we finally went to bed around 10:30 p.m. I got up around 6:30 a.m., had some breakfast, and drove to work at the shop. At noon I decided to let everyone go home because of the snow storm. I stayed for about a half hour to finish a job I was working on.

When I left work I got onto Powell Avenue traveling east and got onto Highway 76. I intended to take the expressway east to town and get off at Elm Street which is a left exit. The snow was coming down real heavy and it took me about an hour to get to where the accident happened. Visibility was poor because there was also a lot of wind. I would estimate that I was going about 30 mph on the expressway because of the weather conditions. Most of the other cars were going at about the same speed.

As I got to where the train station (30th Street) exit is, I slowed down to about 20-25 mph because that's a bad curve and the traffic enters on the left. I was in the right lane. At that time I saw a car which I now know to be Mr. Barber's come up quickly behind me. It was a Cadillac. The Cadillac changed lanes to the left-hand lane and passed me about 100 yards before the train station exit. I would estimate that he was doing about 40 mph. I remember thinking that he was going way too fast for that part of the expressway with those weather conditions.

---

* The transcript of Mark Dennison's deposition was excerpted so that only his answers are reprinted here. Assume that this is a true and accurate rendering of those answers.

Anyhow, after he passed he sort of pulled over to the right but was still in the middle of the road. At that time a small red Toyota inched out from the entrance way into the left lane of the expressway. He swerved a little but never left his lane. The Cadillac hit its front left into the rear right of the Toyota and pushed it hard into the wall. The Cadillac ended up stopped in the middle of the expressway about 175 yards beyond the left-hand entrance past where the Toyota ended up.

I stopped my car, which is a YR-3, Mazda to try to help the guy in the Toyota. I had received emergency first aid training in the Army and worked as a volunteer emergency vehicle attendant for our neighborhood group. I helped the driver of the Toyota, who I now know to be Mr. McLain, out of the car. He seemed shook up but all right except for his right wrist which he was holding on to. No, he didn't complain about any back injury. He seemed to be in a lot of pain but appeared to be concerned about the stuff he had in the back of his car. The car was loaded to the ceiling with cardboard boxes. He also was saying something about his wife and kid.

I took Mr. McLain back to my car and called for a wrecker for his car and the cops on my car phone. About fifteen minutes later both the cop and the wrecker showed up. I gave the cop my name and address and told him what happened. The cop took McLain to the hospital. I remember seeing Mr. Barber talking to the cop. He seemed real upset, pissed off. I don't know why. The accident was his fault.

I told the wrecker to take the car to Kirsch, but it looked like a total to me. It turned out that the rear and the front end damage to the Toyota was substantial, and that the frame was snapped, so it couldn't be repaired. The blue book value on that car was $5,800. We sold it for McLain for parts and gave the money to his insurance company. The boxes in the Toyota turned out to be full of cups, bowls, and other pottery. Except for a few cups that McLain told us we could keep, it was all busted up.

Since the accident I have had some contact with Mr. McLain about his car. About three weeks after the accident I received a complete set of eight pottery coffee mugs from Mr. McLain, thanking me for helping him out on the day of the accident.

I've marked the diagram to show what I saw, and it is accurate. (See Dennison Deposition Exhibit 1.)

I have read the deposition and it contains all I remember about the accident.

(After the deposition was transcribed, it was signed by the deponent, Mark Dennison.)

Certified by:

ANN E. HALL
Certified Shorthand Reporter

Dennison Deposition Exhibit 1

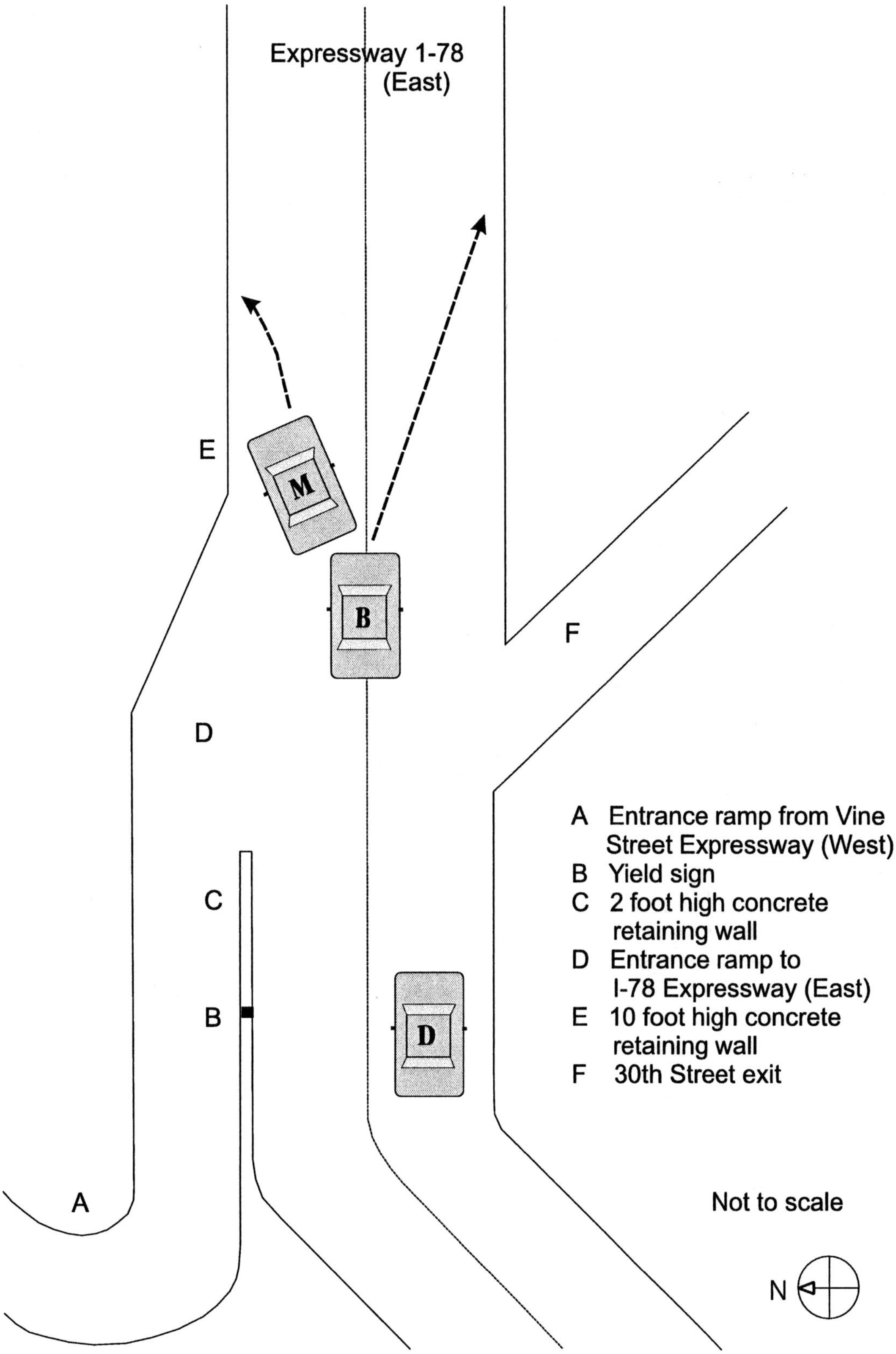

## DEPOSITION OF OFFICER DOMINIC FUSCO*

My name is Dominic Fusco, and I work as a patrol officer for the Nita City Police Department. My badge number is 914. I am 28 years old, married to my wife Angela for the past six years, and we have one son, Louis, who is four.

I grew up in Nita City. After I graduated from high school I went to Nita University and in YR-7 got my degree in Criminal Justice. Since that time I've been with the department. I work as a patrol officer. I've taken the sergeant's exam and each time have been found qualified. I should get promoted in the next year because I've worked my way to the top of the seniority list.

I was working the day shift on February 11, YR-2, the day of the big snow storm. I was patrolling the area of the 30th Street train station. At about 1:30 p.m. I received a call to go to U.S. 76 at the Vine Street entrance eastbound to investigate an accident. The snow had been coming down for a while and there was some accumulation, but the main problem was the wind. This was the third accident of what would be about twenty that I investigated before I finally got off at midnight.

When I got to the scene I found a YR-2 Cadillac that was owned and operated by Mr. Alexander Barber stopped in the middle of the expressway blocking traffic. I instructed him to pull off to the right so traffic could move again. There was some damage to the front left of the Cadillac, but it was still in safe operating condition.

I also found a YR-3 red Toyota owned and operated by Mr. Dennis McLain of Williamstown, Nita. The car had extensive right rear and front left and left side damage and was not operable. A tow truck had apparently been called because it got there at about the same time I did. The Toyota, which was a lift back, was packed with cardboard boxes from the front seat to the back of the car.

I ascertained that the Toyota had entered the U.S. 76 East from the Vine Street entrance on the left. The Cadillac had been traveling at a high rate of speed for the conditions (35-40 mph) down the center of the two lane expressway, hit the Toyota, and forced it into the wall. Damage and resting places of the two vehicles are consistent with this version. I have marked the diagram to illustrate my testimony. (See Fusco

---

* The transcript of Officer Fusco's deposition was excerpted so that only his answers are reprinted here. Assume that this a true and accurate rendering of those answers.

Deposition Exhibit 1.) It is consistent with the diagram on my police report. (See Fusco Deposition Exhibit 2.)I determined that Mr. McLain, who was sitting in a witness's car, had sustained an injury to his right wrist. He appeared to be in pain and rather confused and upset. He reported no other injuries other than to his wrist. I later transported him to the Nita Memorial Hospital Emergency Room.

The driver of the Cadillac, Mr. Barber, was originally belligerent. I told him to wait in his car which he did after moving it to the right side of the expressway as instructed. I later took his name, address, and insurance information and sent him on his way.

I also took down the names and addresses of several witnesses and drew a diagram for later reference in filling out my report. I then took McLain to the hospital. No citations were issued because my primary concern was to get traffic moving and clear the expressway, but the accident appeared to be clearly the fault of Mr. Barber.

I admit that my report is sketchy, but I said I worked until midnight. That was because many officers on the 4-12 shift couldn't make it in because of the snow. I investigated and filed reports on twenty accidents for my duty time that day (16 hours). Therefore they were all bare-bone reports. I do remember this accident because of its location and the fact that I transported McLain to the hospital. During the ride to the emergency room he was quiet but obviously in pain. I do remember his mentioning his wife and daughter but no specifics of the conversation.

I have read a transcription of my deposition and it is true, complete, and accurate.

(After the deposition was transcribed, it was signed by the deponent, Officer Dominic Fusco.)

Certified by:

Ann E. Hall

ANN E. HALL

Fusco Deposition Exhibit 1

Fusco Deposition Exhibit

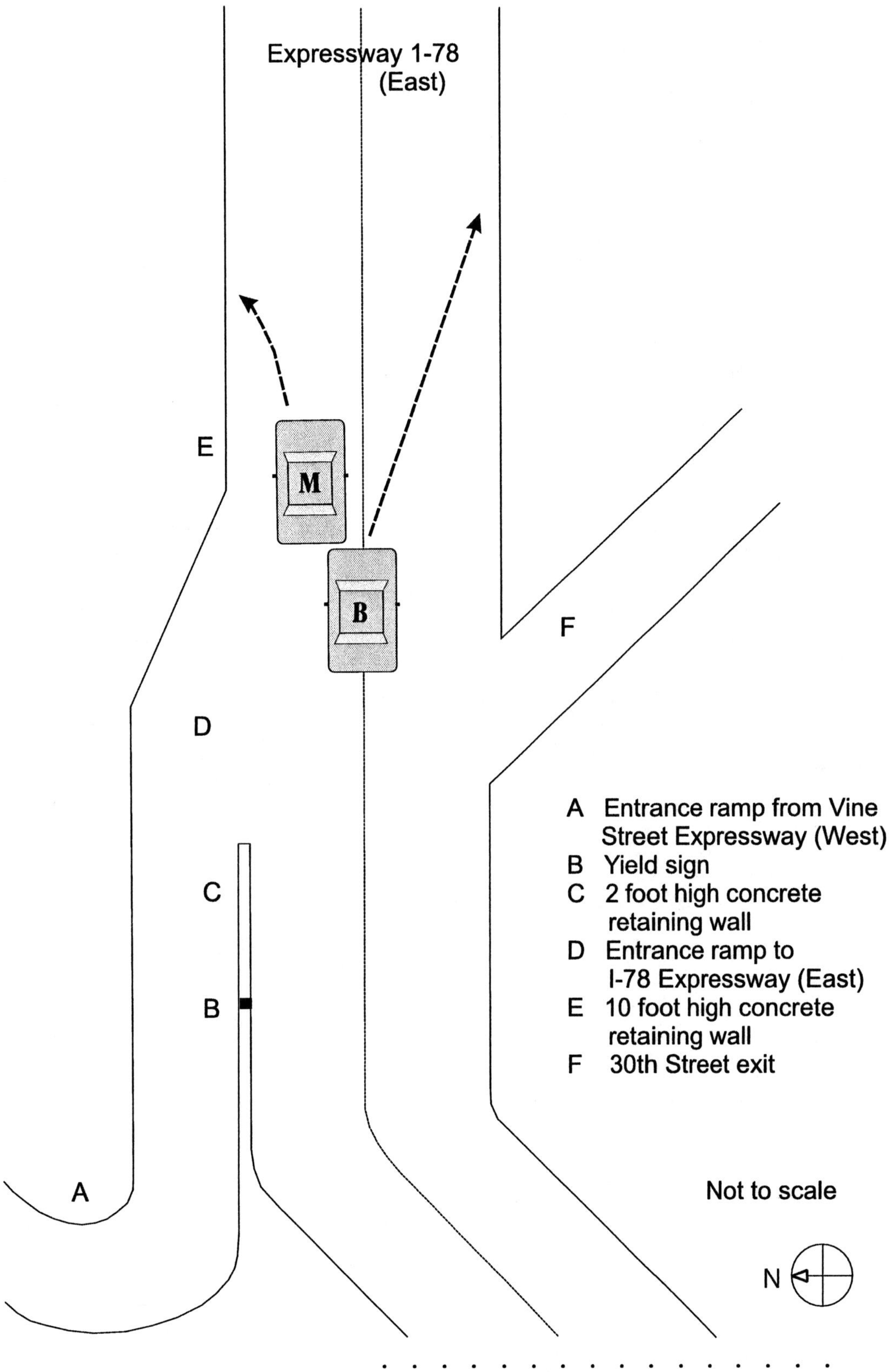

Fusco Deposition Exhibit 2

| DEPT. OF TRANSPORTATION<br>BUREAU OF SAFETY PROGRAMMING AND ANALYSIS<br>T & S BUILDING, NITA CITY, NITA | **POLICE ACCIDENT REPORT** | REPORTABLE ☐<br>NON-REPORTABLE ☐<br>HAZARDOUS MATERIALS ☐ |
|---|---|---|

| 1. INCIDENT NUMBER | 2. AGENCY NAME | 3. STATION PRECINCT |
|---|---|---|
| 0717 | Nita City Police Department | 12th |

| 4. INVESTIGATING OFFICER | BADGE NO. | 5. DATE OF REPORT | 6. APPROVED BY | 7. DATE APPROVED |
|---|---|---|---|---|
| Dominic Fusco | 914 | 2/12/YR-2 | Tanford | 2/14/YR-2 |

| 8. DATE | 9. DAY | 10. TIME | 11. COUNTY | 12. CODE | 13. PATROL ZONE |
|---|---|---|---|---|---|
| 2/11 | Friday | 1:30 pm | Nita | 01 | |

| 14. NO. VEHICLES | 15. NO. KILLED | 16. NO. INJURIED | 17. MUNCIPALITY | 18. CODE | |
|---|---|---|---|---|---|
| 2 | 0 | 1 | Nita City | 01 | 7 |

**UNIT NO 1**

| 19. OPERATOR LICENSE NO. | CLASS | 20. STATE | 21. SEX | 22. D.O.B. | 23. LEGALLY PARKED | 24. ILLEGALLY PARKED | 25. HIT & RUN |
|---|---|---|---|---|---|---|---|
| 0685461 | 1 | VA | M | 7/31/YR-29 | | | |

| 26. NAME | ADDRESS |
|---|---|
| Dennis McLain | 1414 Winding Way Williamstown, NI |

| 27. OWNER NAME | ADDRESS |
|---|---|
| Dennis McLain | 1414 Winding Way Williamstown, NI |

| 28. VEHICLE TITLE NO. | 29. YEAR | 30. MAKE | 31. MODEL | 32. REGISTRATION NO. | 33. STATE |
|---|---|---|---|---|---|
| V174H11232 | YR-3 | Toyota | Liftback | DMP777 | NI |

| 34. INSURANCE CO. NAME | 35. INSURANCE CO. CODE | 36. INSURANCE POLICY NO. |
|---|---|---|
| Travelers | 59 | 7417AP74 |

| 37. TOWED TO | 38. TOWED BY |
|---|---|
| Kirsch Chev. West Nita | Jimmy's Towing |

**UNIT NO 2**

| 19. OPERATOR LICENSE NO. | CLASS | 20. STATE | 21. SEX | 22. D.O.B. | 23. LEGALLY PARKED | 24. ILLEGALLY PARKED | 25. HIT & RUN |
|---|---|---|---|---|---|---|---|
| 4477138 | 1 | PA | M | 7/7/YR-41 | | | |

| 26. NAME | ADDRESS |
|---|---|
| Alexander Barber | 501 Pine Street Nita City, Nita |

| 27. OWNER NAME | ADDRESS |
|---|---|
| Lynn Barber | The Dorchester, Fulton Square Nita City, Nita |

| 28. VEHICLE TITLE NO. | 29. YEAR | 30. MAKE | 31. MODEL | 32. REGISTRATION NO. | 33. STATE |
|---|---|---|---|---|---|
| 3438H71GM114 | YR-2 | Cadillac | Seville | TDP 705 | NI |

| 34. INSURANCE CO. NAME | 35. INSURANCE CO. CODE | 36. INSURANCE POLICY NO. |
|---|---|---|
| State Farm Mutual | 46 | 425-3865-271 |

| 37. TOWED TO | 38. TOWED BY |
|---|---|
| N/A | N/A |

| 39. DESCRIPTION OF DAMAGED PROPERTY: | 40. OWNER |
|---|---|
| | |

| PRINCIPAL ROAD | | | INTERSECTING ROAD | |
|---|---|---|---|---|
| 41. ROUTE NO. OR STREET NAME | 42. SPEED LIMIT | 43. CIRCLE IF ONE WAY | 44. ROUTE NO. OR STREET NAME | 45. SPEED LIMIT |
| U.S. 76 East | 50 | N S (E) W | Vine St. ent. 76 E. | 15 |
| IF NOT AT INTERSECTION | 46. NEAREST CROSS ROUTE OR MILEPOST NO. | 47. DIR. FROM ACCIDENT SITE | 48. DISTANCE FROM ACCIDENT SITE | 49. WAS DISTANCE ☐ MEASURED? ☒ ESTIMATED? |
| | Vine Street Entrance | N S (E) W | 20 feet | |

| 50. ILLUMINATION | 51. WEATHER | 52. ROAD SURFACE | 53. TRAFFIC CONTROL DEVICE TYPE |
|---|---|---|---|
| 2 | 3 | 4 | PRIN ROAD: 0; INT ROAD: 4 |
| 1. DAWN OR DUSK<br>2. DAYLIGHT<br>3. DARK (ST. LIGHTS ON)<br>4. DARK (NO ST. LIGHTS) | 0. NO ADVERSE CONDITIONS<br>1. RAINING<br>2. SLEET, HAIL, ETC.<br>3. SNOWING<br>4. FOG, SMOKE, ETC.<br>5. RAINING AND FOGGY | 1. DRY<br>2. WET<br>3. MUDDY<br>4. SNOW OR ICE | 0. NO CONTROLS<br>1. FLASHING TRAFFIC SIGNAL<br>2. TRAFFIC SIGNAL<br>3. STOP SIGN<br>4. YIELD SIGN<br>5. RR CROSSING CONTROLS<br>6. POLICE OFFICER OR FLAGMAN<br>7. FLASHING SCHOOL ZONE SIGN<br>8. OTHER |

| 54. WITNESS(ES) NAME | ADDRESS |
|---|---|
| Steve Petersen | 120 Almur Drive, West Nita, Nita |
| Mark Dennison | 940 Christian, Nita City, Nita |
| Jeremy Brown | 6304 Drexel Road, Nita City, Nita |

| 55. INJURED TAKEN TO: | BY: |
|---|---|
| Nita City Memorial Hospital | Investigating Officer |

56. USE CODES ON OVERLAY SHEET TO COMPLETE BLOCKS A THRU N OF THIS SECTION

| A | B | C | D | E | F | G | NAME | ADDRESS | H | I | J | K | L | M | N |
|---|---|---|---|---|---|---|---|---|---|---|---|---|---|---|---|
| 1 | 1 | M | 29 | 3 | 9 | 0 | Dennis McLain | 1414 Winding Way Williamstown, Nita | U | 3 | 03 | 05 | B | 8 | 0 |
| 2 | 1 | M | 41 | 3 | 9 | 9 | Alexander Barber | 501 Pine Street Nita City, Nita | U | 0 | - | - | A | 0 | 0 |

Fusco Deposition Exhibit 2 (cont.)

57. DIAGRAM

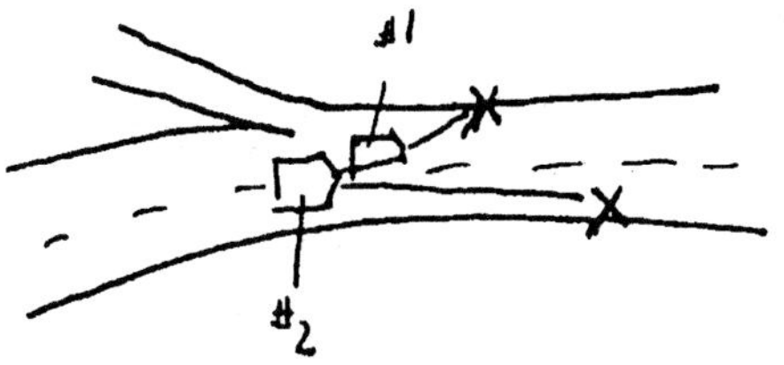


INDICATE NORTH

USE ARROW

Number of Lanes on Principal Road:

58. NARRATIVE

#1 Entered 76 E from Vine Street
Expressway #2 hit right rear of #1
with front left of #2 – #1 driven
into wall. #1 towed
#1 driver taken to Emergency Room of
Nita City Memorial Hospital
#2 drivable
No citations – accident unavoidable

67. VIOLATIONS INDICATED UNIT NO. 1

68. CITATION(S) UNIT NO. 1

69. VIOLATIONS INDICATED UNIT NO. 2

70. CITATION(S) UNIT NO. 2

INCIDENT NUMBER:

VEHICLE NUMBER

| 1 | Field | 2 |
|---|---|---|
| 04 | 59. AUTO/TRUCK BODY TYPE<br>01 - CONVERTIBLE<br>02 - 2 DR HARDTOP<br>03 - 4 DR HARDTOP<br>04 - 2 DR SEDAN<br>05 - 4 DR SEDAN<br>06 - STA. WAGON<br>07 - LIMOUSINE<br>08 - OTHER AUTO<br>09 - JEEP, ETC.<br>10 - PICK-UP<br>11 - VAN (NOT MOVING VAN OR HORSE VAN)<br>12 - TOW TRUCK<br>13 - OTHER SINGLE UNIT TRUCK<br>14 - TRACTOR (CAB ONLY)<br>15 - TRACTOR TRAILER<br>16 - OTHER TRUCK BODY | 04 |
| 06<br>01 | 60. INITIAL POINT OF IMPACT<br>00 - NONE<br>07 - TOP<br>08 - UNDERCARRIAGE<br>09 - TOWED UNIT<br>99 - UNKNOWN<br>01 02 03 07 04 05 06 | 01 |
| 3 | 61. VEHICLE DAMAGE SEVERITY<br>0 - NONE<br>1 - LIGHT<br>2 - MODERATE<br>3 - SEVERE | 1 |
| 1 | 62. WAS TOWING REQUIRED?<br>0 - NO<br>1 - YES | 0 |
| 99 | 63. ESTIMATED TRAVEL SPEED<br>00 - NONE (STOPPED/PARKED)<br>01-97 - CODE ACTUAL SPEED<br>98 - 98 OR GREATER<br>99 - UNKNOWN | 45 |
| 1 | 64. VEHICLE GRADIENT<br>1 - LEVEL ROADWAY<br>2 - UPHILL<br>3 - DOWNHILL | 1 |
| 00 | 65. SPECIAL USAGE<br>00 - NONE<br>01 - PUPIL TRANSPORT<br>02 - FIRE VEHICLE<br>03 - AMBULANCE<br>04 - OTHER EMERGENCY VEHICLE<br>05 - STATE POLICE VEHICLE<br>06 - DOT VEHICLE<br>07 - OTHER STATE GOV'T VEHICLE<br>08 - MUNICIPAL GOV'T VEHICLE<br>09 - OTHER MUNICIPAL GOV'T VEHICLE<br>10 - FEDERAL GOV'T VEHICLE<br>11 - TAXI<br>12 - TOWING CAR<br>13 - TOWING TRUCK<br>14 - TOWING UTILITY TRAILER<br>15 - TOWING MOBILE/MODULAR HOME<br>16 - TOWING CAMPER | 00 |
| 00 | 66. HAZARDOUS SUBSTANCE TYPE - FROM PLACARD<br>00 - NOT APPLICABLE<br>01 - NON-FLAMMABLE GAS<br>02 - COMBUSTIBLE<br>03 - ORGANIC PEROXIDE<br>04 - CORROSIVE<br>05 - EXPLOSIVE "A"<br>06 - OXYGEN<br>07 - POISON<br>08 - EXPLOSIVE "B"<br>09 - CHLORINE<br>10 - OXIDIZER<br>11 - POISON GAS<br>12 - FUEL OIL<br>13 - DANGEROUS<br>14 - RADIOACTIVE<br>15 - FLAMMABLE SOLID -W<br>16 - FLAMMABLE<br>17 - FLAMMABLE GAS<br>18 - FLAMMABLE SOLID<br>19 - GASOLINE<br>20 - BLASTING AGENTS<br>98 - OTHER | 00 |

FOR ALCOHOL TEST TYPES BLOCKS 72 AND 75 USE THE FOLLOWING CODES: 1 - BLOOD 2 - BREATH 3 - URINE 4 - TEST REFUSED 8 - OTHER CHEMICAL

77. IS INVESTIGATION COMPLETE?

| 71. NAME | 72. TYPE | 73. RESULT | 74. NAME | 75. TYPE | 76. RESULT |
|---|---|---|---|---|---|
| | | ____% | | | ____% |

A-45 (9/81)

# POLICE ACCIDENT REPORT

**A** VEHICLE NUMBER:

1 - UNIT NO. 1
2 - UNIT NO. 2

**B** SEATING POSITION:

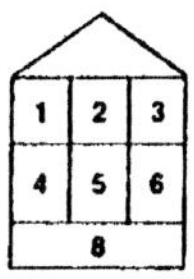


1 - DRIVER
2-6 - OCCUPANTS
7 - PEDESTRIAN
8 - OTHER
9 - UNKNOWN

**C** SEX:

M - MALE
F - FEMALE

**D** AGE:

CODE ACTUAL AGE
CODE 98 FOR 98 OR OLDER
CODE 99 FOR UNKNOWN

**E** ACTIVE RESTRAINT TYPE:

0 - NO RESTRAINTS
1 - SHOULDER HARNESS ONLY
2 - SEAT BELT ONLY
3 - SEAT BELT AND SHOULDER HARNESS
4 - CHILD RESTRAINT DEVICE
7 - HELMET
8 - OTHER
9 - UNKNOWN

**F** ACTIVE RESTRAINT USAGE:

0 - NOT APPLICABLE
1 - IN USE
2 - NOT IN USE
9 - UNKNOWN

**G** PASSIVE RESTRAINT TYPE:

0 - NONE
1 - AIRBAG DEPLOYED
2 - AIRBAG NOT DEPLOYED
3 - AUTOMATIC SEAT BELT
8 - OTHER
9 - UNKNOWN

**H** OPERATOR/PEDESTRIAN DRINKING:

Y - YES
N - NO
U - UNKNOWN

**I** APPARENT INJURY SEVERITY:

0 - NO INJURY
1 - DEATH
2 - MAJOR INJURY
3 - MODERATE INJURY
4 - MINOR INJURY

**J** TYPE OF APPARENT INJURY - MOST SEVERE:

01 - AMPUTATION
02 - BLEEDING
03 - BROKEN BONE(S)
04 - BURNS
05 - CONCUSSION
06 - SHOCK
07 - DIZZINESS
08 - ABRASIONS/BRUISES
09 - COMPLAINT OF PAIN
98 - OTHER

**K** AREA OF APPARENT INJURY - MOST SEVERE:

01 - FACE
02 - HEAD
03 - NECK
04 - BACK
05 - ARM(S)
06 - LEG(S)
07 - CHEST/STOMACH
08 - INTERNAL
09 - ENTIRE BODY
98 - OTHER

**L** INJURY INFORMATION SOURCE:

A - OBSERVATION OF OFFICER
B - STATEMENT FROM INDIVIDUAL
C - MEDICAL/PARAMEDICAL PERSONNEL

**M** EJECTION:

0 - NOT APPLICABLE*
1 - TOTALLY EJECTED
2 - PARTIALLY EJECTED
3 - PARTIAL EJECTION INVOLVING EXTRICATION

EXTRICATION BY:

4 - UNKNOWN PERSON (S)
5 - TWO OR MORE TYPES
6 - AMBULANCE/RESCUE
7 - POLICE
8 - OTHER
9 - UNKNOWN*

*APPLIES TO BOTH

**N** EMERGENCY MEDICAL SERVICE TYPE:

0 - NONE
1 - COMMERCIAL/PRIVATE UNIT
2 - MUNICIPAL/VOLUNTEER UNIT
3 - HOSPITAL BASED UNIT
8 - OTHER
9 - UNKNOWN

CODE THE LETTERED COLUMNS BELOW USING THE CODES DESCRIBED IN THE CORRESPONDING LETTERED BOXES ABOVE

| A | B | C | D | E | F | G |

| H | I | J | K | L | M | N |

United States Weather Bureau

Weather Summary
Almanac

The following climatological data is the official report of the United States Weather Bureau for the city of Nita City, Nita, during the week of February 6, YR-2.

Sunday February 6, YR-2

Temperature: High 42° low 27°
Precipitation: 0 inches
Daylight Sky Conditions: 65% Cloudy

Monday February 7, YR-2

Temperature: High 45° low 24°
Precipitation: 0 inches
Daylight Sky Conditions: 80% Sunshine

Tuesday February 8, YR-2

Temperature: High 39° low 22°
Precipitation: 0 inches
Daylight Sky Conditions: 95% Sunshine

Wednesday February 9, YR-2

Temperature: High 37° low 21°
Precipitation: 0 inches
Daylight Sky Conditions: 100% Sunshine

Thursday February 10, YR-2

Temperature: High 33° low 27°
Precipitation: 0 inches
Daylight Sky Conditions: 98% Cloudy

Friday February 11, YR-2

Temperature: High 34° low 31°
Precipitation: 16.8" of snow (from midnight thru midnight)
Daylight Sky Conditions: 100% Cloudy

Saturday February 12, YR-2

Temperature: High 37° low 30°
Precipitation: 6.9" of snow (from midnight thru midnight)
Daylight Sky Conditions: 65% Cloudy

**Uniform Arrest and Disposition Record**

| | |
|---|---|
| Name: | Dennis McLain |
| S.S. No.: | 323-46-3818 |
| D.O.B. | 7/31/YR-31 |
| P.O.B.: | Williamstown, Nita |

| Date | Offense | Disposition |
|---|---|---|
| YR-8 | Felony Possession of Marijuana | 3 Months in County Jail Williamstown, NI |

George McDonald
Superintendent of Documents
Commonwealth of Nita

Charlotte Noll
Notary Public
Comm. Expires: 2/23/YR+2

# MICHAEL A. GRATCH, M.D.

Practice limited to
Orthopaedic Surgery
25 Lendough Avenue
Williamstown, NI 50505
732-7200

June 23, YR-1

Diane Restler
Attorney for Plaintiff, Dennis McLain
1 Liberty Place
Nita City, Nita

RE: *McLain v. Barber Case*

Dear Ms. Restler,

You have asked that I review the records of the above named individual. I should note at the outset that I rarely, if ever, become involved in aspects involving litigation as I find them time consuming, bothersome, and of no academic import. I have nonetheless agreed to review these records and offer my expert opinion regarding the ultimate outcome of this individual as we have a long-standing relationship, and I genuinely believe that his life has been severely compromised owing to this unfortunate accident.

As you can see from my office records which are supplied, I have known this individual since he was a young man. Without being repetitious it is sufficient to say, based on my office records, that this individual has had a long-standing history of asthma, often requiring the use of steroid medication. While this is an outstanding medication for the treatment of asthma in the severely compromised individual, it nonetheless does have certain drawbacks, especially in terms of slowing healing of fractures as well as causing some individuals to be fracture prone. While the patient has shown on occasion a tendency toward slower healing rate, his recovery results have always been outstanding and without compromise. I have always found him to be a compliant individual and concerned about maximizing his recovery potential.

Regarding this accident, the patient suffered a Colle's fracture of the right arm on February 11, YR-2. Owing to great anxiety and concern, given his past medical history, he preferred to see me instead of an unknown physician. The three-day delay in therapy really made no difference as regards to the healing of the fracture as he was more than adequately immobilized with a soft splint. His healing progress was certainly adequate and after removal of the cast he was begun on an intensive rehabilitative program.

Though experiencing some personality conflict with his therapist, the patient made more than satisfactory progress for an injury of this sort. A review of his overall progress at the Lenow Institute reveals an excellent therapy program with good home care. This was certainly a frustrated individual as his livelihood depends on the good motor skills of his fine muscles of the right hand and left hand. Loss of coordinate activity with one or the other hand in an artist can be fatal in terms of an ultimate recovery. In his urgency and desire to resume a normal existence, the patient occasionally entertained activities that might have been dissuaded in the conservative approach. Nonetheless, I found that his activities never extended beyond the point of reasonability and can see nothing in his rehabilitative effort that could have compromised his ultimate result.

As is unfortunately the case in fractures of this type, there are a certain number of patients who will never again regain 100% function of the affected area. This may be especially so in artisans and musicians who require a very highly developed motor skill that the average individual would never miss after such an injury. In addition, a lack of coordinate activity between right and left, as is present here, is a prime deficit for an artisan such as Mr. McLain. Although in some cases there is a return of fine motor skill and coordination, many individuals will never resume their normal level of activity. I would also note the unfortunate result of contracture which is almost always definitively seen in situations of severe trauma as was the case with this patient. Very often these contractures will stabilize, but they can also become far worse. I have discussed the possibility of surgery to resolve this situation, but as of now the patient demonstrates a severe fear of surgery and opts to avoid it at this time.

I would conclude by stating that the patient's resultant wrist injury and residual dysfunction are most certainly a result of this unfortunate accident.

This patient also suffered an injury to his back in this car accident. Examination of this patient relative to his back injury reveals the following:

Patient has a history of back injury, dating from June 6, YR-6, when he injured himself lifting a box of pottery and was evaluated including a myelogram. This injury healed without residual problems. Since that time the patient has injured his back occasionally in either his profession as a potter or in recreational sports, but never sustained any significant injury. There is no family history of back problems.

The patient states that despite the passage of time and fifteen heat and massage therapy sessions, he is still symptomatic. He complains of low back pain with radiating dysesthesiae into his left leg and occasionally into his right thigh. There is a variation of the extent of the radiculopathy, but at times is goes down to the calf.

The patient, who used to be a potter, cannot perform the type of physical activity necessary for that profession. He feels that he has to confine himself to less physically demanding activity. The patient attempts to exercise as best he can, but his physical capacity, despite his attempts, is significantly limited.

On examination the patient is 6'0" tall and weights 172 pounds. The patient carries himself well but is clearly protecting his lumbar spine. There is no sign of overt muscle fasciculation, atrophy, or tremor.

June 23, YR-1

Finger-to-finger, thumb-to-thumb, heel-to-toe, and Romberg tests are negative. Reflexes are 2+ and bilaterally symmetrical at biceps, triceps, brachiordialis, patella, and Achilles. Toes are downgoing. Straight leg raising and Lasegue tests are positive on the left. Faber test is negative. Adson's, Wright's, and reverse Phalen's tests are negative bilaterally in the upper extremities. Motor strength is well within the normal range in all major motor groups.

Range of motion of the cervical spine is 95% of normal. Thoracolumbar range of motion is 90% of normal. The patient reports pain and has to move very slowly over the last 25% of motion. When asked to do repetitive spinal flexion and extension, the patient shows abnormalities of lumbar rhythm. These findings are reproducible.

herniated disk

Review of MRI revealed moderate to large herniated disc at L4-L5 and L5-S1 as well as stenosis of the spinal canal which is not revealed on the lumbar myleogram.

Patient suffered a herniated disc L4-L5 which is pre-existing from YR-6, however, the accident in YR-2 contributed to the injury of the back with the possibility of additional protrusion, making the patient symptomatic. Conservative heat and massage treatment, together with the use of ibuprofen and robaxin, have failed to resolve the problem.

At this juncture there is very little that can be done for this patient. I have recommended that he continue his heat and massage therapy, so long as it provides some relief. Surgery has been discussed but is really not an option at this time. Patient has been advised to avoid any activity involving heavy lifting or prolonged periods in a standing or seated position.

little that can be done

I would conclude by stating that the patient's current back injury was clearly caused by the accident on February 11, YR-2. Any preexisting back problems had been resolved before this accident, and the patient was essentially asymptomatic.

I have included my fee for service and curriculum vitae as requested. As per my usual understanding these fees will be remitted to the Children's Hospital of the Williamstown University Medical Center under my aegis.

I hope that I have answered your questions sufficiently.

Sincerely,

MICHAEL A. GRATCH, M.D.

MAG:ew

Enclosures

MICHAEL A. GRATCH, M.D.

Practice limited to
Orthopaedic Surgery
25 Lendough Avenue
Williamstown, NI 50505
732-7200

NEW PATIENT HISTORY

RE: Dennis McLain
Updated as of February 14, YR-2

PAST MEDICAL HISTORY

Denies Diabetes Mellitus, T.B., Rheumatic Fever, Center. (+) history of epilepsy (currently inactive), strong history of asthma since childhood (intermittent therapy with theophylline derivative, steroid derivative).

Surgical History unremarkable (see accompanying office records regarding orthopaedic history).

Allergies - none (other than asthma-related conditions).

SOCIAL HISTORY

Artisan, works with pottery.
Married.
Currently nonsmoker, prior history one pack per day, stopped YR-5.

FAMILY HISTORY

Father (alive); age 61; history positive for high blood pressure, Reynaud's syndrome (currently in remission).
Mother (alive); age 59; medical history essentially unremarkable.
Siblings, brother (alive); age 26, medical history unremarkable.

LABORATORY DATA TO DATE

Complete blood count (CBC)
WBC - 11,000 (Neuts - 76%, L-20%, Eos. -7%)
H/H = 15/40.3
U/A - Sp. grav. 1.012, WBC's - 2 to 4, Prot. - Neg., Ket. - Neg., RBC's - Neg., Bact. - Few, Hyaline Casts - Trac.
SMA - 12 (Chem. profile) - essentially within normal limits, ANA/LE prep./equivocal (read as normal, "reevaluate in future for better correlation").

# MICHAEL A. GRATCH, M.D.

Practice limited to
Orthopaedic Surgery
25 Lendough Avenue
Williamstown, NI 50505
732-7200

**OFFICE RECORDS**
**PROGRESS NOTES**

RE: Dennis McLain

| DATE | NOTES |
|---|---|
| Jan. 8, YR-17 | 14-year-old male referred by Dr. Stern (family physician) following bicycle accident whereupon patient fell forward when his bike jammed, landing on left side without outstretched left arm. Patient seen by me in emergency room in Williamstown Community Hospital, where x-rays revealed a buckle fracture of the distal radius on the left arm. This required simple casting with sling. Follow-up visit two weeks. |
| Jan. 22, YR-17 | Patient doing well without complaints. Mother notes cast soggy in places owing to difficulty in bathing. Cast removed and recasted for convenience. Continue present routine and return to office in four weeks. |
| Feb. 24, YR-17 | X-ray reveals complete healing of fracture site. Cast removed. Mother instructed as to proper physical therapy at home in order to rebuild arm strength. Anticipate no difficulty resuming normal activity within two weeks. Return to office one month. |
| Mar. 23, YR-17 | Arm well healed. Appears to be functioning normally. Discharged from cast. |
| Nov. 17, YR-14 | Patient seen in emergency room in Williamstown Community Hospital for leg pain following tennis match. Apparently patient had severe asthma attack (history of asthma since age 8), stumbled during attack, and fell on right side. Now complaining of severe pain lower right leg. Note medications for asthma include Theophylline 3 times a day, Vanceril inhalant P.R.N., and recent use of Prednisone 5 mg. T.I.D. for asthma. Exam reveals point tenderness over right lateral malleolus. X-ray reveals hairline fracture right fibula near epiphyseal plate. Ankle-thigh cast employed. Anticipate 8 weeks cast with walker within one month. Return to office in two weeks. |

| | |
|---|---|
| Dec. 2, YR-14 | Patient doing well. X-ray reveals good healing at this time. Some concern regarding proximity to epiphyseal plate. Conservative therapy maintained. Return to office in three weeks. |
| Dec. 23, YR-14 | Recasted in cast room at Williamstown Community Hospital. Walking cast employed. Maintain current regimen. Return to office in one month. |
| Jan. 24, YR-13 | X-rays appear to demonstrate good healing. Noted that patient on high doses of Prednisone for recurrent asthma attacks. Will maintain casting approximately 6 more weeks to insure maximum healing. Some concern regarding osteoporotic activity secondary to medication. Return to office one month. |
| Feb. 23, YR-13 | Cast removed and instruction for physical therapy given to parents. Recommend intensive physical therapy times 2 months at the Lenow Institute of Outpatient Rehabilitation of the Hospital of the Williamstown University. Return to office two months. |
| Apr. 26, YR-13 | Leg strength almost normal. X-rays reveal complete healing. Physical therapy successful. May resume normal activities as desired. |
| Apr. 10, YR-11 | Patient wishes an office visit to discuss soreness in right ankle. Past medical history reviewed and physical exam unrevealing. X-rays appear within normal limits. Explained to patient that there may be some residual arthritic changes secondary to fracture.<br>Encouraged to resume full activities as desired. Reassurance given. Norgesic Forte P.R.N. for ankle discomfort. |
| May 12, YR-11 | Patient called office. Noted much improvement in ankle. Does not request further appointments at this time. |
| Jan. 27, YR-6 | Patient comes to office with back spasms in the lower back region. Notes onset of discomfort following heavy lifting of pottery boxes in studio. No prior history of back pain noted. Full examination with straight leg lifts reveals no sciatic nerve impingement.<br><br>HEAD - normocephalic.<br>NECK - supple<br>CHEST - no rib tenderness, lungs clear to ascultation and percussion.<br>CARDIAC - regular sinus rhythm.<br>BACK - no C.V.A. pain or tenderness noted. Point tenderness L4/L5 region, probably secondary to lumbosacral strain.<br>MYLEOGRAM - Positive for<br>Herniation at L4-L5. |

EXTREMITIES - UPPER - reveal normal reflex activity. Good arm strength bilaterally. Small nodules noted on right palmar eminence area 4th and 5th digit. Appear unremarkable. Probably benign.
EXTREMITIES - LOWER - unremarkable. Suggest rest and conservative therapy.
Patient will receive heat and massage therapy and return in two - three weeks.

Feb. 18, YR-6

Patient returns for follow-up examination. Back pain has lessened but problem continues. Patient will continue heat and massage therapy as needed and return in four weeks.

Mar. 19, YR-6

Patient is without persistent back pain. Notes that minor pain returns with long periods of time in a seated position. Recommend stretching exercises and use of ibuprofen should symptoms return. Follow-up appointment scheduled for one month.

April 17, YR-6

Patient calls to cancel appointment - Reports that his back problems have resolved and that he has been pain-free for several weeks.

Feb. 14, YR-2

Patient present with emergency room record from Nita City Memorial Hospital with a diagnosis of Colle's fracture of the right radius. Patient was struck by automobile in the rear of his car while attempting to get onto the expressway during a very snowy day. Suffered multiple contusions and injury to right wrist. Apparently hand was outstretched on the column of the steering wheel and as such took full impact of the collision. Patient notes extreme anxiety at the time of the accident, in general, dissatisfaction with the emergency room personnel whom he found to be insensitive and nonattentive. Patient indicates that he felt attending physician made inferences about alcohol consumption, which were unfounded. Apparently blood alcohol level was drawn, which was within normal range. For this reason, patient decided not to seek further therapy regarding the fractured wrist and indicated his desire to be treated in Williamstown. His arm was immobilized in a soft splint. X-rays today reveal a minimally displaced simple Colle's fracture. After intravenous injection of Valium, moderate traction exerted in order to maximize bone placement whereupon a convolution-type wrist-elbow cast applied. Anticipate 4 weeks with cast followed by two weeks with simple below elbow cast. Patient very anxious regarding vocational skills. Patient reassured that the fracture is not a complicated one and that good rehabilitative therapy should maximize the healing chances.

| | |
|---|---|
| Feb. 28, YR-2 | Patient doing well, no problems. Cast appears to be functioning properly. Return to office two weeks. Patient reports persistent back pain, at times radiating down left leg and into right thigh, not controllable by use of ibuprofen. MRI performed. Positive for herniated disc L4-L5, L5-S1. |
| Mar. 10, YR-2 | Cast removed. Fracture line appears well healed. Smaller cast placed for two more weeks duration. |
| Mar. 24, YR-2 | Fracture site appears completely healed. Cast removed and patient referred for physical therapy to begin next week. Instructions for physiotherapy utilizing hydro massage for home use until physical therapy can begin. Patient notes difficulty with business scheduling. Notes that he will begin physical therapy as soon as possible. Back problems persist. Massage and heat therapy recommended. |
| May 3, YR-2 | Patient doing very well. Actively pursuing physical therapy as recommended. Will maintain contact with the Lenow Institute of Outpatient Rehabilitation. Physical therapist in charge, Ms. Linda Rosen. |
| June 26, YR-2 | Patient appears very anxious and upset with physical therapist. Notes that she appears impatient with his approach to exercise skills. Notes that she seems unsympathetic with discomfort he encounters after full range of motion exercises. Patient also feels that physical therapist is implying that he does not take his exercises seriously enough. Wife present with patient and she corroborates his anxiety regarding his physical therapy visits. Will contact Ms. Rosen and strongly emphasize that continued pressures will only discourage the patient. Will ask that she comply with my present exercise instructions at the regular time intervals recommended prior. |
| Aug. 26, YR-2 | Patient appears to be doing much better. Seems more relaxed. Back problems somewhat resolved, but some residual persistent pain. Patient would like to engage in some limited contact sports with summer nearing an end and a holiday weekend approaching. Patient reassured that most likely such activity would normally be acceptable but that owing to prior history of slightly delayed healing and resolving back problem, would recommend conservative approach of avoiding all contact sports at least until fall. Thus, I would recommend the conservative approach of avoiding baseball, football, soccer, and recommend swimming at best. |

| | |
|---|---|
| Nov. 10, YR-2 | Spoke to Ms. Rosen regarding rehab. effort of patient. Believe that termination of regular exercise program is acceptable owing to patient's desire to terminate as well as practical feeling that home care would be more than adequate at this point. Ms. Rosen questions presence of nodules on palmar surface of right hand. Indicated to her that these present at least since Jan., YR-2, and represent benign changes and probably of no concern. |
| Jan. 20, YR-1 | Patient doing well but somewhat concerned about stiffness in right hand, especially with limited mobility of the 3rd, 4th, and 5th digits. Notes that over the holidays he had very good digital mobility and almost maximal hand strength but that this has diminished in the last month. Feels very depressed that his progress is going the wrong way. Heat treatment given and has to return to clinic in one month. Suggests maintenance of home exercise. Persistent back pain resolved. Pain returns with prolonged periods of sitting or standing, or with vigorous physical exercise. |
| Feb. 23, YR-1 | Hand strength essentially unchanged. Still noting difficulty with gripping on certain days. Nodules in 4th and 5th fingers somewhat more emphasized on palmar aspect. Beginning to represent picture of Dupuytren's Contracture. Maintain home care and will follow on a monthly basis. |
| Mar. 22, YR-1 | Patient cancels appointment due to scheduling conflict. |
| Apr. 24, YR-1 | Contracture more prominent. Gripping strength adequate but fine digital movement very compromised. Suggested surgical alternative with patient, who seems somewhat anxious about invasive procedures at this time. Prognosis for a full recovery seems guarded at this point. |

## LENOW INSTITUTE OF OUTPATIENT MYOPATHIC REHABILITATION

Hospital of the Williamstown University

| DATES | PROGRESS NOTES |
|---|---|
| 4/20/YR-2 | 29-year-old male referred by Dr. M. Gratch for intensive physical therapy of the right wrist after recent auto accident resulting in Colle's fracture with median nerve involvement and ulnar nerve impingement of a minor degree resulting in compromised motor function and coordinate delicate movement relative to left side. Dr. Gratch requests standard Lenow protocol involving strength enhancing exercises of the entire wrist, as well as particular development of the lumbrical and dorsal interosseous musculature owing to patient's occupation in the arts. Fracture was apparently uncomplicated and required no open reductions. Arm was immobilized six weeks in the standard wrist-elbow position and demonstrates good healing at the fracture site on x-rays taken 4/7/YR-2. Patient was unable to begin therapy until this time owing to scheduling difficulties on his part. As such, sessions will continue 15 minutes longer than the standard forty-minute spacing. This will continue times 2 months when the regular schedule will supervene. Dr. Gratch has agreed with this plan. |
| 4/23/YR-2 | Gripping strength tested for baseline right hand at 22 Feldman units*, left hand at 45 units (normal range). Range of motion routine explained and instituted with supervision. Patient complains of severe pain on digital palmar flexion and supination maneuvers. Stressed that this is not unusual early in therapy and the importance full compliance with procedure. Pat. understands. |
| 5/4/YR-2 | Good range of motion exercise efforts today. Strength test same. Whirlpool and diathermy Rx. |
| 5/7/YR-2 | Full range motion, fine muscle development exercises, whirlpool and diathermy as per last visit. |

* A Feldman unit is a generic term used to measure relative hand strength.

# LENOW INSTITUTE OF OUTPATIENT MYOPATHIC REHABILITATION

Hospital of the Williamstown University

| DATES | PROGRESS NOTES |
|---|---|
| 5/11/YR-2 | Full Lenow protocol (i.e., range of motion exercises with fine muscle skill development of lumbrical and dorsal interossei muscle groups) as per regular routine. Pat. left twenty minutes early c/o "headache." |
| 5/14/YR-2 | Appointment cancelled. |
| 5/25/YR-2 | Will begin to space visits soon. Dr. Gratch called and suggested increasing whirlpool treatment and diathermy treatments. Patient tested for strength and notes moderate improvement to 24 Feldman units. Sessions to run forty minutes as of next visit. |
| 5/28/YR-2 | Session included routine range of motion procedures. Patient requests omitting heat therapy due to schedule conflict. Given home exercise instruction sheets for introduction of home exercise program in conjunction with clinic schedule. To involve 20 minutes of range of motion skills, ten minutes of which will include fine muscle exercises. (Pat. indicates he had piano at home—have encouraged repetitions of scales in one octave as this is an excellent exercise for the development of fine muscle skills—this is highly recommended, but optional.) |
| 6/8/YR-2 | Full session with heat therapy at conclusion. Patient expressing dissatisfaction with progress. Told that these things take time, but good improvement will come in many cases when the original injury is a simple fracture, as was the case with patient. Reassurance given and again emphasis placed on joint clinic and home care. |
| 6/11/YR-2 | Strength test unchanged. Routine procedures. |
| 6/22/YR-2 | Wrist strength improved at 28 Feldman units. Fine motor development essentially unchanged. |

## LENOW INSTITUTE OF OUTPATIENT MYOPATHIC REHABILITATION

Hospital of the Williamstown University

| DATES | PROGRESS NOTES |
|---|---|
| 6/25/YR-2 | 20 minute session—patient c/o headache. Appears very angry and impatient. Does not vocalize well. Claims home exercises are tiresome and boring. Will suggest to Dr. Gratch possibility of increasing visits to twice weekly for one month and resuming regular routine after that. |
| 6/28/YR-2 | Strong letter from Dr. Gratch suggesting that increasing visits will only discourage patient. Requests that further such suggestions be held to a minimum. |
| 7/6/YR-2 | Routine range of motion exercises without pain noted. Patient apparently not doing optional home exercises as admitted, finding them of "no value." Skipped whirlpool Rx. |
| 7/9/YR-2 | Cancelled appt. (no show). |
| 7/20/YR-2 | Full range of motion exercises with some discomfort. Notes that he has "missed a few days of home exercises." Strength unchanged in hand. |
| 7/23/YR-2 | Good session today. Routine exercise program YR-2 w/o difficulty. |
| 7/27/YR-2 | Regular routine. Strength improved to 32 Feldman units. Notes increased dexterity in fine motor activity. Coordinate strength unchanged. |
| 8/3/YR-2 | Pat. encouraged with motor skill improvement. Whirlpool treatments only as pat. had business appt. |
| 8/10/YR-2 | Routine program. Progress essentially slow and steady. Reemphasize diligent home care to patient. |
| 8/17/YR-2 | Routine program gripping skills improving, dexterity markedly improved. Pat. notes better compliance with home exercise program, even suggesting that piano exercise makes a difference. |

## LENOW INSTITUTE OF OUTPATIENT MYOPATHIC REHABILITATION

Hospital of the Williamstown University

| DATES | PROGRESS NOTES |
|---|---|
| 8/24/YR-2 | Routine program. Continue per routine. Dr. Gratch sent updated progress report. |
| 8/31/YR-2 | Short visit without heat therapy or fine muscle exercises performed. |
| 9/7/YR-2 | Some discomfort in hand. Admits to playing baseball over holiday weekend against advice of Dr. Gratch. Use only heat and whirlpool therapy today. |
| 9/14/YR-2 | Called to cancel owing to illness. States he will still perform his home exercises. |
| 9/21/YR-2 | Wife called to cancel. Noted car trouble. Wife seemed unsure what I meant about home skills exercises. |
| 9/28/YR-2 | Thirty minute appt. Seems to perform exercises with moderate difficulty. Seemed angry when asked about compliance with home exercises, "Ask me, not my wife...I'm the one with the bum hand, not her!" |
| 10/5/YR-2 | Routine skills exercises. Full therapy today. |
| 10/12/YR-2 | Short visit, omit whirlpool and diathermy. Strength improved to 38 Feldman units. |
| 10/19/YR-2 | Cancelled appt. c/o headache. Spoke to supervisor. |
| 10/26/YR-2 | Routine visit. Noticeable strength improvement. Fine muscle development increasingly improved, though noticeable difficulty with "finger spreading," i.e.—still limited dorsal interossei ability. |
| 11/2/YR-2 | Asking to terminate protocol and remain only on home care. After full session, informed patient that this would have to be discussed with Dr. Gratch. |

**LENOW INSTITUTE OF OUTPATIENT MYOPATHIC REHABILITATION**

Hospital of the Williamstown University

| DATES | PROGRESS NOTES |
|---|---|
| 11/9/YR-2 | Routine session. |
| 11/10/YR-2 | Spoke to Dr. Gratch regarding slowing of program and Dr. Gratch feels that home exercise may be just as beneficial at this point in the rehab. effort. He feels that there may well be residual of some amount on a permanent basis. Discussed question of nodules on palmar surface of right hand just under fourth and fifth digit at proximal area to hand. Dr. Gratch has noted these since last January, YR-2, and felt they were benign. |
| 11/16/YR-2 | Routine visit. |
| 11/26/YR-2 | Cancelled appt. |
| 11/30/YR-2 | Final regular appt. Will schedule as desired on monthly basis. Told to maintain rigorous home care, though pat. seemed somewhat unenthusiastic about the need for this. Will continue under care of Dr. Gratch. |

## Anatomy of the Hand

### Bone Structure of the Hand and Wrist

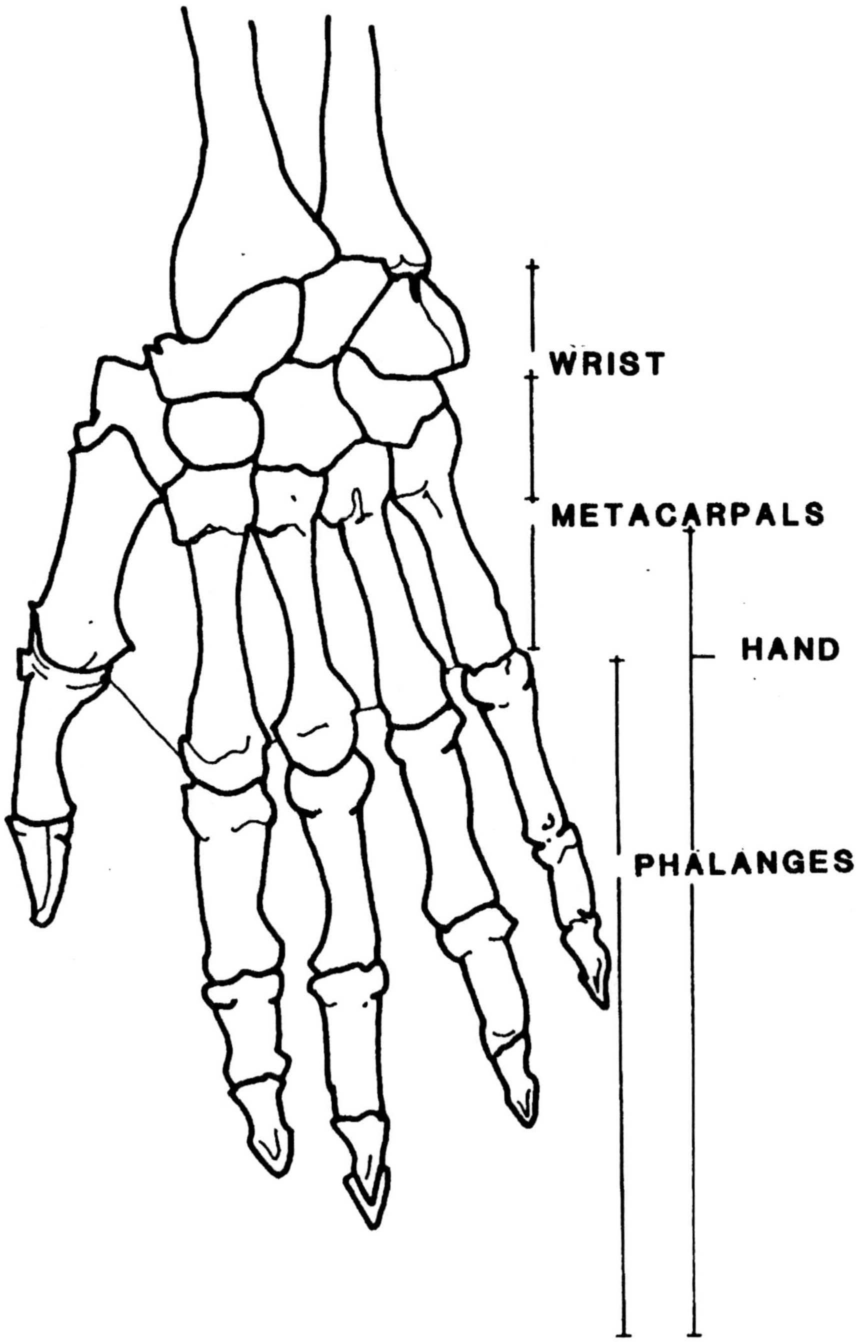

Emergency Room Report

| | | |
|---|---|---|
| PATIENT'S NAME<br>McLain, Dennis | DATE-<br>2/11,YR-2 | McLain<br>54-32-734 |
| PATIENT'S STATEMENT- struck from behind by another vehicle while entering expressway going east from Vine Street. Brought by police. Feels achy all over with much pain in right wrist. | | PHONE-<br>(505)542-8331 |
| PATIENT'S SIGNATURE- Dennis McLain | | TIME-<br>1:49 P.M. |
| ADDRESS- 1414 Winding Way<br>Williamstown, Nita | ALLERGIES- NONE | MARITAL STATUS -<br>Married |
| INSURANCE NO. - BC/BS<br>6789-436-2098 | SOC. ~~SEC~~ -<br>271-55-3056 | RELIGION -<br>N/A |

PHYSICIANS'S NOTATIONS 332-46-3818

1:55 p.m. 29-year-old male noted to have been struck from behind by Cadillac and thrust into concrete barrier in his Toyota. Reports no loss of consciousness, generalized aches, and pain right wrist region. Past medical history positive for epilepsy (inactive x 7 years) and asthma (controlled) since childhood. Denies recent alcohol consumption. No other passengers in vehicle—Patient. Brought by ambulance by Nita City police from accident site (U.S. 76 East); police report no unusual behavior by patient.

Pulse rate and vital signs stable. WD/WN male somewhat anxious but oriented. Contusion left lower mandibular areas. Contusion left shoulder. Moderate swelling right knee. Neurologic status intact with CN's II-XII intact, nl, reflexes Dilate upper + lower. Chest-clear, Heart-NSR at 90/m; no M noted; And -nl.; Flank-non tender, chest-no pain in area ribs Exts - right wrist with "silver Fork"; deformity - good finger mobility.

Physician's Orders: X-ray skull, neck, chest, flat plate, right and left knee, right hand, right wrist with left-sided comparison. CBC, V/A, Blood A/Ch.

2:55 p.m. Films negative except Colle's fracture right wrist. Minimal fracture line, minimally displaced. Labs negative (-). Blood alcohol--.058 (legal).

Plan: Admit to hospital, set right wrist in cast, continue to observe. Patient refused admission; wants to see own physician in Williamstown. Advised patient of need for immediate casting. Set + splint.

CONDITION ON DISCHARGE -

IMPROVED _____ UNIMPROVED _____ OTHER Signed out against medical advice!

| | | |
|---|---|---|
| SIGNATURE OF PHYSICIAN<br>Rachel McKaplan M.D. | ROOM # IF ADMITTED- | INSTRUCTIONS- See Dr. Gratch A.S.A.P. Keep wrist immobile.Tylenol. |

Exhibit—X-ray

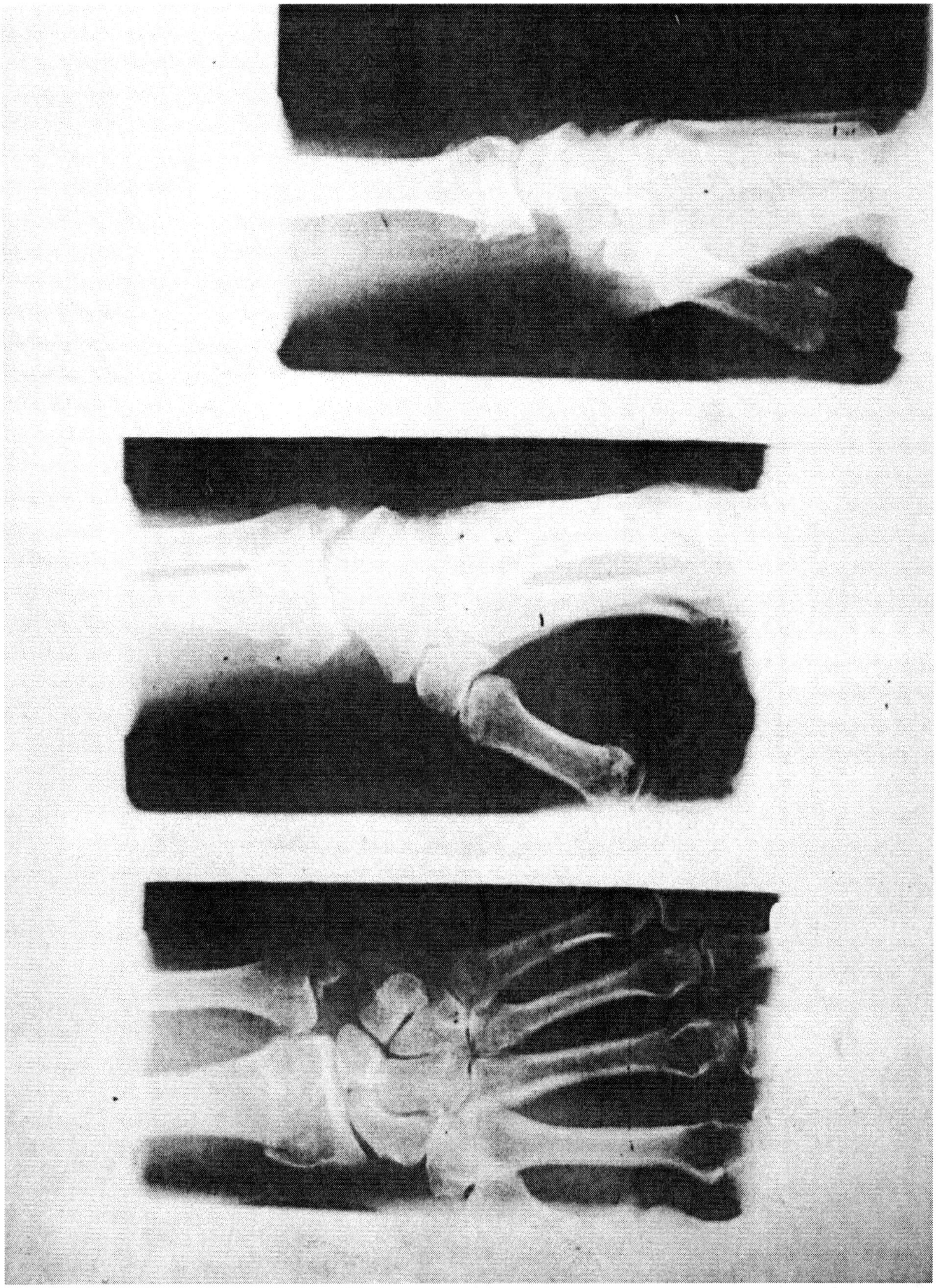

## MICHAEL A. GRATCH, M.D.

---

Practice limited to
Orthopaedic Surgery
25 Lendough Avenue
Williamstown, NI 50505
732-7200

June 23, YR-1

Diane Restler
1 Liberty Place
Nita City, Nita

Re: Dennis McLain

For Professional Services Rendered

Three (3) hours at $250.00 per hour = $750.00

Please make check payable to Children's Hospital of University of Williamstown (note source).

Thank you.

Michael A. Gratch, M.D.

**DEPOSITION OF JEAN VITALI, M.D.***

My name is Jean Vitali. I am a medical doctor specializing in psychiatry. (See attached curriculum vitae).

I am testifying at the request of my patient Dennis McLain concerning his current psychological problems for which he is being treated. He is suffering from depression as the direct result of  injuries received in an automobile accident in February YR-2.

Mr. McLain presents a classic case. To understand the depth of his condition it is important to understand his history. Because of the history, Mr. McLain is suffering from depression to a greater degree than would normally be anticipated with injuries such as he presents.

Mr. McLain is a thirty-one-year-old white male. He was born and raised until his early teens in Scottsville, Nita. He is the oldest of two siblings. His brother, David, is a medical doctor currently serving an internship at Massachusetts General Hospital in Boston. His parents are retired. His father was an engineer. His mother was a secretary and homemaker.

Mr. McLain was reared in a normal middle class home. In YR-28, when he was three years old, his parents had just purchased their first home. At that time both parents were working—an apparent economic necessity. Dennis was cared for during working hours at a daycare center. At that time his mother became accidentally pregnant with David who was born in YR-27.

This unplanned child provided an additional economic hardship for the family when Dennis's mother was forced to take a leave of absence from work. Marital difficulties also developed between his parents. Mother, faced with the caretaking responsibilities of two children in addition to the economic hardship, became increasingly short-tempered with and withdrawn from Dennis, who, at age four, managed to get into things typical for a child of his age. Most of his mother's attention was directed toward the new baby, David. Dennis, therefore, could no longer get what he wanted either emotionally or materially.

Perceived neglect in his early years played a significant part in his tendency to doubt his personal worth. Denial of parental attention made his struggle for adequacy more

* The transcript of Dr. Vitali's deposition was excerpted so that only her answers are reprinted here. Assume that this is a true and accurate rendering of those answers.

difficult. Pained by this form of abandonment, he became vulnerable to feelings of dependency and depression. This is one of the frequent beginnings of depression; one in which the individual begins to suspect that he is not "good" enough to gain and maintain parental love. This is probably the case with Dennis, though it is not possible to state this with certainty.

As the two boys matured, Dennis's low evaluation of himself and probable self-hate continued. His brother, David, was an excellent student and as Dennis puts it, "The apple of his mother's eye." Dennis tried to succeed in nonacademic ways. Efforts at athletic powers were thwarted by asthma and a tendency to suffer fractures after overexertion due to medication necessary to control the asthma. His brother meanwhile excelled not only in academics but in athletics. (He attended and graduated from Harvard University, where he was captain of the football team. He also attended Harvard Medical School.)

In YR-13, Dennis entered college at the University of Williamstown. He reports that his parents pushed him to attend an Ivy League school but that he was denied admission. He attended the University of Williamstown, even though he would have preferred going to school away from home, because it was the only school to accept him.

While in college Dennis experimented heavily in drugs while he pursued a fine arts degree. While in college he found success in his pottery work and an increased sense of self-esteem. At the time he was experiencing his first success in his art work, he met and courted his eventual wife, Jennifer.

Since graduating from college, Dennis has enjoyed a good deal of success, receiving many awards for his work. His art work provided the basis for his self-esteem. Prior to his injuries he had developed a good family relationship with his wife and child and the couple had achieved a good deal of financial success. Of this, Dennis was very proud.

When Dennis injured his wrist and his back he developed a fear of having lost all his means of achieving status, livelihood, and a secure financial place alongside his brother. These feelings are heightened by the fact that ten months prior to the accident he and his wife had purchased a new home. The perceived loss of self-esteem was substantial and caused a reactivation of early loss during early childhood years when his mother directed her attention to the new, talented sibling in the household. There was even fear that by being handicapped (as Dennis refers to himself) his wife and child would not respect or love him because he was no longer able to achieve his hard-earned status as an artist and good home-provider.

As you know from my report, I have been treating Mr. McLain for six weeks. He has made good progress, but I anticipate that he will require at least another six months of twice-a-week sessions. His progress, however, is good.

I have brought my current billing for Mr. McLain. (See McLain Deposition Exhibit 4.)

I am being compensated for my time at this deposition by Mr. McLain's attorney. My fee for deposition is $1,000. Should it become necessary to testify at trial my fee will be $2,000 for trial preparation and trial testimony.

It is true that I have testified for the plaintiff's attorney in six previous cases over the past three years. None of these patients or Mr. McLain were referred to me by plaintiff's counsel. I do end up in court on many occasions because I have developed a specialty in treating post-traumatic depression. My income from expert witness fees usually amounts to $30-$35,000 per year which represents approximately one-quarter of my income.

(Assume that Dr. Vitali produced the report at the deposition and it is consistent with testimony.)

I have read this transcript of deposition and it is true and accurate.

Jean Vitali, M.D.

Certified by:

ANN E. HALL
Certified Shorthand Reporter

# Jean Vitali, M.D.

| | |
|---|---|
| Address: | 410 Medical Arts Building<br>Williamstown, Nita |
| Education: | Bucknell University, B.S. Chemistry, Magna Cum Laude, YR-19<br>Duke University Medical Center, M.D. YR-16<br>General Internship, Duke University Medical Center, YR-16 to YR-14<br>Psychiatric Residence, Massachusetts General Hospital, YR-14 to YR-10 |
| Licenses: | North Carolina, Massachusetts, Nita |
| Board Certification: | American Board of Psychiatry and Neurology, YR-10 |
| Professional Experience: | Private Practice, Limited to Psychiatry, Williamstown, Nita, YR-10 to present<br>Assistant Professor of Psychiatry Williamstown University Medical College, YR-6 to present<br>Qualified as an expert witness in the field of Medical Science and Psychiatry in the State and Federal Courts of Nita on 80 occasions in both civil and criminal cases. |
| Publications: | "Post Traumatic Depression in Automobile Accident Cases," *New England Journal of Medicine*, January, YR-2.<br>"Depression, the Normal Response to Physical Injury," *Nita Medical Bulletin*, YR-4.<br>"Physical Injury and Resulting Mental Illness," *Nita Medical Bulletin*, YR-5. |
| Professional Societies: | American Medical Association<br>Nita Medical Association |

## DEPOSITION OF ALEXANDER BARBER*

My name is Alexander Barber. I am 43 years old. I was born in Nita City on July 7, YR-43. I graduated from Nita City High School in YR-25 and Nita University in YR-21, where I received a B.A. in Business Administration, *magna cum laude*. I married Lynn Riley in YR-11, and we have two great kids, Richard and Helen. Rich is 8 years old and Helen is 5 years old.

In YR-7 we moved into a townhouse at 5th and Pine in Society Hill where we have lived ever since. It is a nice place to live and really, it makes me proud of what I've done. The kids are doing well with Rich in private school and my little Helen going to an advanced kindergarten school. Those kids are amazing—they seem so smart for their ages. In August, YR-3, my wife and I separated, but the two kids live with me along with a nanny who takes care of them when I'm not around. I put my wife in an apartment in Fulton Square until we work things out. Since we separated, she is working again as a legal secretary for a Center City firm and is attending Nita University Law School as an evening division student.

I own two cars personally which don't belong to the business. I have a Pontiac Trans Am which is black with gold decals. It is a stick shift, four-speed. I bought a Cadillac Seville to celebrate the opening of my West Nita store. However, I transferred the ownership of the Cadillac to my wife, Lynn, in YR-2. After our separation she needed a car, so I gave her the Caddy and got insurance in her name with State Farm. My agent recommended I put everything in her name so someone couldn't sue me if she was in an accident. I do own some real estate. About three years ago I bought my parents a new home in the Northeast. The title is in my name. I have one lot in Society Hill with four other lots in Nita Village which is a new area of development near Society Hill. I own a condo in Cape May, Nita, which is right on the beach. The kids have trust accounts of about $50,000 each which is for their education. The accounts are at the First Trust Bank. That is where I banked when I was at Nita University, and they helped me with the business. I pay myself a salary of $250,000 a year, but the rest of the earnings are put right back into the business. I have my auto insurance with the Travelers Insurance Company. I have two policies. The first one, I.D. #567834, has $300,000 aggregate coverage for personal injury and property damage. The second one, I.D. #835768, is what they call an umbrella which is worth two million dollars. My wife's policy is with State Farm, policy #425-3865-271.

* The transcript of Barber's deposition was excerpted so that only his answers are reprinted here. Assume that this is a true and accurate rendering of those answers.

After going to Nita University, I was accepted at the Business School at Nita University, but I figured I had done enough stuff on theory and I wanted to get out and get my hands dirty. I went to work at J.C. Penney's in Nita in YR-20 as an assistant manager of the sporting wear division. In YR-18 I moved over to Sears as assistant manager of all sport lines and soon became the manager of the entire sporting goods division.

In YR-12 I decided to go into business myself. I saw from my work at the other two stores that there was a big market for a multipurpose sporting goods store. I sell bicycles, athletic shoes, sports gear, and clothing for all types of sports. I have to admit that I was lucky in that I decided to go into the business for myself at the time when Nita City had decided to rebuild the Center City—Society Hill area of downtown. I took a chance and applied for federal, state, and city financing to renovate two buildings. One was on South Street and the other on Chestnut Street near Fulton Square.

I opened two stores in YR-12 with the name Athletics Unlimited, Inc. I am the sole shareholder of the corporation. It is hard to know what it is worth, but taking the inventory, buildings, and all other things together, I would figure it is worth 7-9 million dollars. Again, I was lucky in many ways in starting my business back then. Everybody was getting into sports and Nita was booming with new businesses downtown. My operation grew by leaps and bounds, and I opened new stores in Nita City, Nita, Northeast Nita City, South Nita near Nita University, and North Nita by Nita State University. I also have a store down in Wilmington, Nita, which is doing great.

I have continued to grow and my newest store is in the West Nita Mall, just to the northwest of Nita off of U.S. 76 West. This is where I was coming from on February 11, YR-2, the day of the accident. It takes a lot of work to get a new store going and for the last six months before the accident I drove from my house to the mall on a daily basis. I normally took 4th Street down to Lombard, went West on Lombard Street to U.S. 76, and headed west on 76. I would usually take the same way home every day, except I'll go east on Elm Street. Once in a while I would go north on 5th to the Vine Street Expressway and then get on U.S. 76.

I have a very clear memory of the day of the accident. The reason why is that I was planning a big sale that weekend at the West Nita Store. I got Raleigh bikes and Nike running shoes because I can buy in great volume for all of my stores. I had decided to sell them at cost at the West Nita store and at retail at all of the others. I thought that my "Summer Sale" in February would get the people into my new store and hopefully they would become regular customers in the future.

I had been working hard that entire week because of the sale. I was putting in about 14 to 16 hours a day. That is not too different than my usual for I normally work about 12 hours a day. On Thursday night, the 10th of February, YR-2, my wife came over to see the kids. I came home about 9:00 p.m., and we had a few glasses of sherry together while we were talking. I think I had four drinks which were about the size of a wine glass. The alcohol made me sleep well even though I normally have no trouble sleeping. I went to bed around midnight so I got my normal five hours of sleep.

I got up very early that morning, around 5:00 a.m., so I could drive out to the store to get ready for the sale. I would start that day on Friday, February 11, and would go until Sunday evening. I drove my new Cadillac Seville because I wanted a heavy car because they predicted snow. My Trans Am was too powerful for slick roads and would slide all over. My wife had left the Caddy at my house. My wife is affected by alcohol quite easily, and I didn't want her to drive home that night after drinking the sherry. So, I got her a cab and gave her money to go home and enough to take a cab in the morning to come pick up her car. I told her if she didn't stop by, I would bring the car over after work on Friday. On Friday, I decided to drive it to work and drop it off on the way home. I told the nanny to call Lynn later in the morning. I don't know if she ever did call her.

I got to the store by 6:30 a.m. and worked hard all morning to get ready for the sale. By noon, I knew the sale was off. It had begun to snow and they predicted one to two feet. I couldn't believe it was happening to me after spending thousands of dollars on advertising and overtime pay for the employees. I got really mad, but I was really just so disappointed that all of the work was for nothing. I called the Nita City Gazette to see if they could pull my ads for Saturday and Sunday, but they had already started printing.

My employees wanted to leave at noon because the radio had said that, weather bureau and police were telling everyone to go home. All the other stores in the mall were closing for the weekend so I decided to let everyone go home. I decided to get home and check on the kids.

I left the store and headed out on 76 East for Nita City. The snow was really coming down, and I remember that the flakes were really big. The wind was very strong, and it looked like there was already a lot of snow on the ground. However, the pavement on the highway was basically clear because of the heavy traffic and the wind. It was slow going, but traffic moved at around 40 mph. It was slick, but there was enough traction to stop. Traffic was heavy to the Powell Avenue exit, but it was lighter from there to downtown. I could go about 45 mph to downtown.

I planned to take the Vine Street exit but traffic was backed up. So I decided to go by the 30th Street exit and get off on Elm Street, my usual route home. I can't say what speed I was going at the time of the accident, but it couldn't have been more than 30 to 35 mph. I know I had slowed down because traffic always gets backed up in this area. I went by Vine and headed east in the right-hand lane of U.S. 76. As I got close to the 30th Street exit, my lane of traffic was basically clear. I noticed there were cars lined up waiting to enter the highway from the Vine Street entrance.

Everything was fine until I got close to the 30th Street exit when out of the corner of my eye I saw something coming at me. A small red foreign car apparently coming from the Vine Street entrance shot out onto the road with its rear end sliding directly into my lane—just a few feet in front of me. There was nothing I could do but hit the brakes. I didn't even have time to turn the wheel. The right rear of the foreign car clipped the left front of my Cadillac. The foreign car slid into the concrete barrier, and my car slid to a stop in the right-hand lane with the front end cocked in a southeasterly direction. (See Barber Deposition Exhibit 1.)

Thank heavens no one hit me from behind. All traffic stopped and a huge traffic jam was caused by this other driver. Before I knew it, the police were there. My car was drivable, but it had about $1,000 worth of body damage. (See Barber Deposition Exhibit 2.) The cop took my name and license number and told me to get going so traffic could start moving. The other driver looked okay and was mumbling something about that he could not see. I wasn't hurt, and I went home to check on my kids. The cop said he'd get back to me about the other driver. I called State Farm and Travelers on Monday to tell them what had happened.

I have read this transcription of my deposition and it is true and correct.

(After the deposition was transcribed, it was signed by the deponent, Alexander Barber.)

Certified by:
Ann E. Hall
ANN E. HALL
Certified Shorthand Reporter

Barber Deposition Exhibit

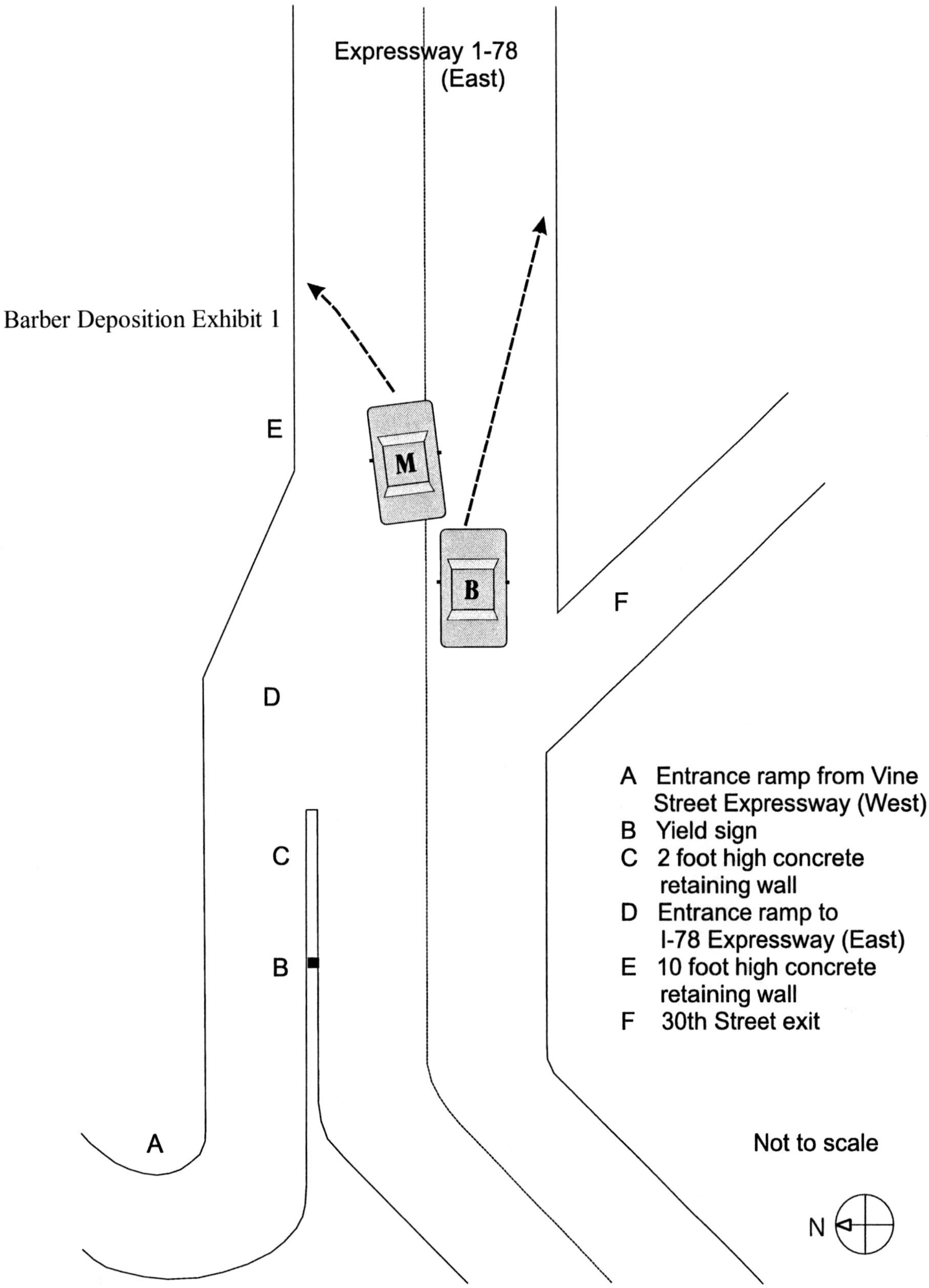

Barber Deposition Exhibit 2

February 22, YR-2 Invoice No: 35789

DON ROSEN CADILLAC CO.
190 Presidential Blvd. North
West Nita City, Nita

| Item | Work Completed | Parts | Labor | Total |
|---|---|---|---|---|
| 1 | LEFT 1/4 PANEL AND | | | |
| | MOUNTING | 395.00 | 75.00 | 470.00 |
| 1 | HEADLIGHT AND FRAME | 42.50 | 22.00 | 64.50 |
| 1 | MICHELEN TIRE | | | |
| | (OLD TIRE SLASHED) | 98.75 | 15.00 | 113.75 |
| 1 | FRONT GRILL AND | | | |
| | MOLDING | 265.08 | 62.00 | 327.08 |
| | | | | |
| | | | | |
| | | | | |
| | | | | |
| | | | | |
| | | | | |
| | | | | |
| | | | | |
| | | | Sub-Total | 975.33 |
| | | | TAX | 7.00 |
| | | | TOTAL | 982.33 |
| | | | | |
| | | | | |

# Driving Safety Record
# State of Nita

Name: Alexander Barber
License Number: 2938415267

| | Violation | Date | Place | Disposition |
|---|---|---|---|---|
| 1. | Speeding | 5/3/YR-7 | Nita City | Fine $25 |
| 2. | Failure to yield right of way | 5/9/YR-7 | Nita City | Fine $45 |
| 3. | Speeding | 5/12/YR-7 | Nita City | Fine $35 |
| 4. | Passing in no passing zone | 12/1/YR-5 | Capital City | Fine $65 |
| 5. | Speeding | 3/9/YR-4 | West Nita | Fine $45 |
| 6. | Speeding | 4/3/YR-3 | Nita City | Fine $100 |

Paul Carrington
Director
Bureau of Records
Motor Vehicle Division of Nita

Sara Sun
Notary Public
Commission Expires YR+4

## DEPOSITION OF JEREMY BROWN*

My name is Jeremy Brown. I have never been called Jerry and prefer to be called Jeremy. I am 27 years old, and I was born October 10, YR-27, in Minneapolis, Minnesota. My parents moved to Nita City when I was five and bought a home in Overbrook which is a neighborhood in Nita City off of Powell Avenue. I still live with my parents at 6304 Drexel Road. I graduated from high school in YR-9, and I am currently attending Nita State University. I took four years off after high school—two years traveling and the other two working for Bekins Moving Company. I am a sociology major with a business minor. I hope to obtain my Masters in Social Work (MSW) at Nita University after graduation.

I did see the accident which happened on February 11, YR-2, on U.S. 76 East. Steve Petersen and I were on our way to the airport at the time the accident happened. I was driving my jeep, and Steve was in the right front seat. We were going to pick up a good friend of ours who had been in Snowmass, Colorado, skiing. The three of us were high school friends. Even though a blizzard had started, I wasn't worried about getting stuck because my jeep has four-wheel drive.

I have a vague recollection of what I did the week before the accident. I really have a strange schedule because of my work. I am usually up and around from 3:00 a.m. until 9:00 or 10:00 p.m. each day. I normally jog about three miles before I go to bed at night, but I hadn't run for three or four days of that week because I had a terrible cold. I do remember going to bed around 7:30 p.m. on Thursday, February 10, YR-2, because I was so tired because of the cold. I wanted to get rid of it. When I got up early Friday morning I was feeling a lot better.

Steve and I both work early mornings. I did get up about 3:00 a.m. as usual to get to work by 4:30. I had some orange juice and a bowl of cereal before I left for work. I work for U.P.S. unloading trucks and Steve for the Postal Service doing the same thing. We both were done about 10:30 or 11:00 a.m. and then we went out for breakfast. I had eggs and a Bloody Mary, and I think Steve had an omelette with a couple beers. We sat around for a long time talking about courses. (Steve is at Nita University in Political Science.) At about 12:15 p.m. we took off for the airport.

I drove up Broad Street from Center City and then took a left onto Vine Street. Vine Street has an entrance onto 76 East.

I headed west on Vine and then took a left onto the entrance to U.S. 76 East toward the airport. The traffic was moving at

* The transcript of Brown's deposition was excerpted so that only his answers are reprinted here. Assume that this is a true and accurate rendering of those answers.

about 15 to 20 mph on Vine Street and even slower on the entrance ramp because of the visibility and the snow already on the road. The entrance is literally a U-turn, and I remember I almost hit the concrete embankment because it was so slick. It was hard to see because of the blowing snow and parts of the road were really covered with snow. After making the turn I had to stop on the entrance because there were three or four cars stopped in front of me waiting to get on U.S. 76. This isn't unusual because this entrance is so dangerous. You have no space to merge on to 76. You have to just jump out onto the highway. (See Brown Deposition Exhibit 1 attached.)

As we waited to enter, a small red foreign car, a Honda, I think, all of a sudden jumped out onto the highway and its back end slid into the right-hand lane of U.S. 76. It was then I saw the Caddy, also in the right lane. There was nothing he could do but hit his brakes. I saw his rear brake lights go on, but it was too late. The Caddy clipped the Honda in the right rear end and the Honda was pushed into the concrete wall. All traffic stopped, and we just sat there.

I got out of the jeep and ran up to see if I could help. The people in front of us did not stop. They just pulled around the accident and went on their way. I noticed that there was glazed ice in the left-hand lane of Highway 76 where the Honda entered. No one seemed to be hurt and a cop came real quickly. I didn't give him my name because I didn't want to get involved. Steven did though, and that is why I am here today. I could see the whole thing because my jeep has large tires and it sits higher than a car. I didn't talk to the driver of the Caddy, but the other driver was complaining about his left wrist and saying he couldn't believe the Caddy swerved into his lane. I think the Caddy was going about 35 to 40 mph at the time of the crash, but I really couldn't tell because I didn't see it for a long time before the impact.

As I've testified, I had one Bloody Mary with breakfast. Also, I never said that the Cadillac was traveling too fast for conditions. The Honda was definitely at fault. The Cadillac never really had a chance.

I have read this transcription of my deposition and it is true and correct.

(After the deposition was transcribed, it was signed by the deponent, Jeremy Brown.)

Certified by:

ANN E. HALL
Certified Shorthand Reporter

Brown Deposition Exhibit

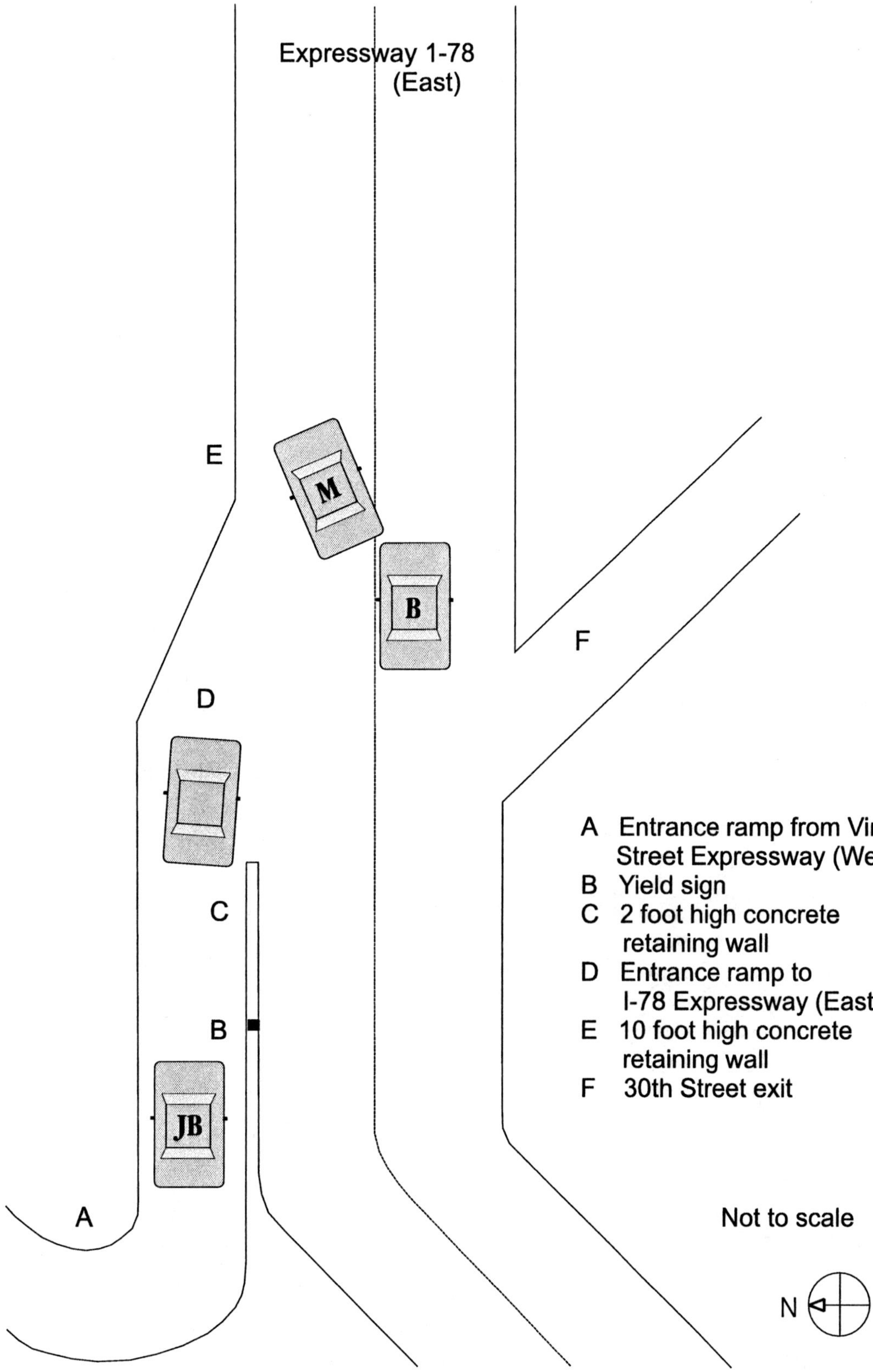

## DEPOSITION OF STEVEN PETERSEN*

My name is Steve Petersen. I am 25 years old, and I was born on April 10, YR-25, in Nita City. I grew up in West Nita, Nita, and I still live there with my parents at 120 Almur Drive. I graduated from high school in YR-7, and I work for the U.S. Postal Service. I attend Nita University part-time, and I am majoring in Political Science. I hope to go to law school at Nita University in their evening division. I used to work full-time for the Postal Service, but now am part-time while I go to school. I work early mornings unloading trucks. I start about 5:30 a.m. and work to about 11:00 a.m.

The week before the accident was a hard one for me. My girlfriend had been in Colorado for two weeks. We had a fight before she left, and I was feeling guilty about it. I hadn't been sleeping well, but I am a light sleeper anyway. I normally get to bed around 11:00 p.m. since I get up early. However, on Thursday, February 10, YR-1, I got to bed about midnight. I had been at the Triangle Tavern in Nita City talking to an old girlfriend of mine. We had a late supper around 10:00 p.m. I think we had a large sausage pizza, and we split a pitcher of beer. I took my friend home and jumped into bed about midnight.

I was with Jeremy Brown when I saw the accident. We are high school buddies. Jeremy and I had breakfast after work that day. He works at U.P.S. unloading trucks. As I said, my girlfriend was coming back from Colorado that day, and Jeremy was nice enough to drive me out in his jeep to pick her up. I don't own a car, and my girlfriend's car has bald tires, so I didn't want to drive it in the snow. We ate breakfast after work in Center City. I had an omelette and orange juice. Jeremy had eggs and a Bloody Mary. I was a little worried about his drinking before driving, but he seemed okay.

We took off for the airport about 12:30 or a quarter to one. Jeremy drove his jeep up 11th Street to Vine. I remember going up 11th because the parked cars were on both sides of the street and it was hard not to sideswipe one with the slick conditions. Jeremy took the Vine Street Expressway to Hwy. 76 East. It sure was slick because there wasn't a lot of snow on the ground yet so the streets were icy. I remember Jeremy almost hitting the concrete barrier at that U-turn on the Vine Street entrance to Hwy. 76. That is always a dangerous turn, even when it is dry. Just as we turned, we met a line of cars waiting to get onto U.S. 76 East. There were about seven cars and a pick-up truck ahead of us.

* The transcript of Petersen's deposition was excerpted so that only his answers are reprinted here. Assume that this is a true and accurate rendering of those answers.

what about the pickup truck

Because the jeep sits higher than most cars, we could see ahead of us. At the front of the line was a red Toyota. I recognized it because I was thinking of buying one like it. It is a liftback with front-wheel drive. Jeremy asked me to stick my head out of the window to see what was holding us up. I think a pick-up truck ahead of us partially blocked his vision. I looked out the window, but it was hard to see because of the blowing snow. I looked ahead and then back to the west at traffic.

The left-hand lane of Hwy. 76 momentarily cleared, and there was a new Cadillac in the right-hand lane. I saw it long enough to estimate it was traveling about 30 to 35 mph. I also noticed it was hugging the center line of the road as the snow was getting heavy on the shoulder. I guess the driver didn't want to catch his right wheels in the drifts. I don't think he ever got out of the right lane, however.

Just as the Caddy got about 25 feet from the Toyota, the Toyota pulled into the left lane, and its rear end slid toward the right lane. I guess it was slick, and the car's front-wheel drive caught dry pavement and swung the back around. I couldn't tell if the Toyota's rear end crossed the center line, but it was sure close. The Caddy hit the Toyota and pushed it into the concrete wall (see Petersen Deposition Exhibit 1). I don't remember seeing the rear brake lights of the Cadillac.

After the accident, traffic came to a complete stop. We both got out and walked forward to see if we could help. I don't really know what Jeremy did. I noticed that in the left lane, just where the Toyota would have pulled out, there were two or three inches of loose snow. It wasn't packed down, but it might have caused the Toyota to spin its wheels a little bit before it caught the dry pavement.

I talked to the driver of the Caddy. I didn't see the driver of the Toyota. The driver of the Caddy made some statement about how he couldn't stop, but he couldn't believe the Toyota slid into his lane. I just checked to see if he was okay and offered to push his car off the road, but he said it was drivable. A police officer came. He apparently drove down the 30th Street exit the wrong way to get down to Hwy. 76. I told him I was a witness and told him what I saw. He took a few notes and then took down my name and telephone number. He then told all of us to get back in our cars so traffic could start moving again. It was then that a tow truck arrived and hauled the Toyota away. I noticed that it had a bunch of boxes in the back of the car and the back seat was down.

I have read this three-page transcription of my deposition, and it is true and correct.

Steve Petersen

Steve Petersen

Certified by:

Ann E. Hall

ANN E. HALL
Certified Shorthand Reporter

Petersen Deposition Exhibit 1

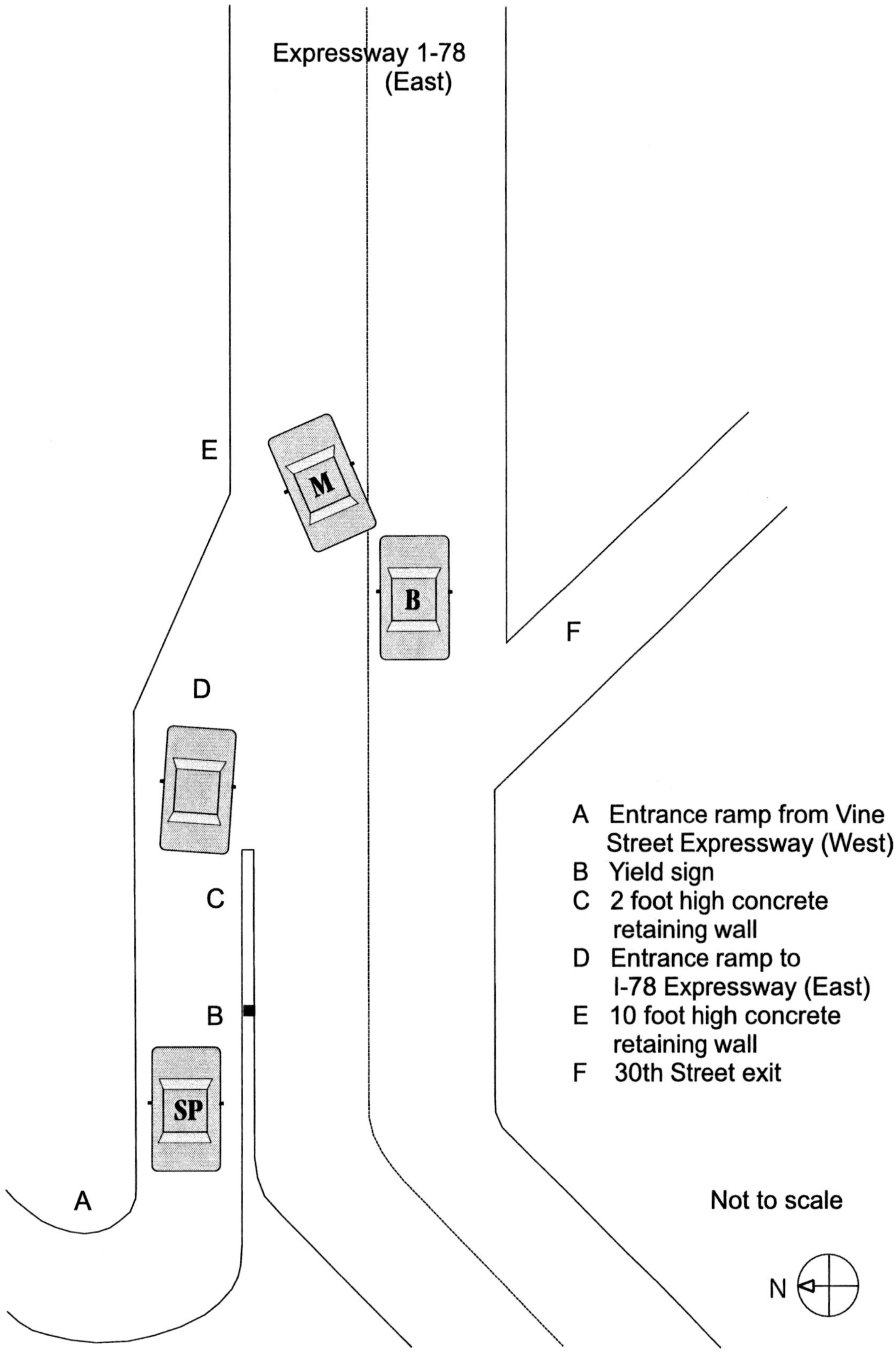

RACHEL M. KAPLAN, M.D.
Greenhill Lane #809
Nita City, Nita

June 15, YR-0

Ronald L. Benton
Attorney for Defendant

Re: Dennis McLain

Dear Mr. Benton:

In response to your request, I have reviewed all pertinent materials regarding the plaintiff and conducted a physical examination of him. I will address myself to both of his claims of physical injury as a result of a car accident on February 11, YR-2. The patient has made claims regarding injuries to both his wrist and his back. I will address the wrist injury first.

I first saw the patient on February 11, YR-2, when patient was brought into the emergency room of the Nita City Memorial Hospital following an automobile accident. At that time, a complete physical exam was performed by myself which revealed multiple contusions of minor variety and one complication to be noted, a fracture of the right wrist identified as a Colle's fracture. Owing generally to the necessity of quick fracture reduction, I strongly recommended admission overnight with follow-up x-rays and immediate casting.

The patient was most reluctant to allow appropriate therapy and signed out of the hospital against medical advice. He did allow a soft cast to be placed at that time. He was informed of the importance of quick and rapid therapy but decided he preferred to see his own physician in Williamstown, Nita. Owing to my prior experience with this individual and also having reviewed the subsequent medical records, I would conclude that the resultant nonhealing difficulties were secondary to the patient's own failure to minimize this unfortunate result. The reasons are as follows:

1. Failure to allow prompt treatment in a fracture of this type will always increase the chances of a poor healing result. I believe that the three (3) day delay that occurred certainly contributed to this ultimate result. In fractures of this type, the displaced bone can often compress the median nerve in the lower arm which feeds several of the digits and offers sensory and motor supply. Often, compression of such a nerve will result in some residual harm unless treatment occurs immediately.

2. Having reviewed Dr. Gratch's office records, it is obvious that the patient had a long-standing history of steroid use and subsequent osteoporotic difficulties secondary to this medication. As a result, this individual was far more prone to fractures than the average individual not using steroid medication. The patient's failure to include this information upon history-taking in the emergency room deprived the medical team of all necessary information by which a proper therapeutic approach could have been achieved.

3. A review of the rehabilitative records at the Lenow Institute shows several indications of patient noncompliance with his rehabilitative effort. I would note an original delay in rehabilitative therapy which immediately caused a compromise. In addition, there seems to be a poor attitude regarding the home care aspects of his treatment. One who uses the fine musculature of the hand, especially in his profession, should be particularly attentive to such highly specialized exercise routines. I would note several canceled appointments which I believe are reflective of a patient unwilling to maximize his chances for recovery. By way of example I would note the September 7, YR-2, notation which indicates that the patient played baseball against medical advice, thus augmenting the stiffness in his hand.

4. It would appear that there is prior evidence of contractures in the palmar aspect of the right hand. Such contractures often present with unknown etiology and can lead to the type of deformity that the patient now exhibits. This would be totally unrelated to any automobile accident which may have occurred subsequent.

I would conclude regarding the wrist injury by saying that any chance for a full recovery was negated by the patient's obvious noncompliance with appropriate medical and physical therapy. In addition, there is strong evidence to suggest that this problem would have occurred regardless of any automobile accident.

I now turn my attention to the plaintiff's claim of back injury as a result of this car accident on February 11, YR-2. I have reviewed all pertinent records regarding this claim, including the results of a myleogram and MRI performed on this patient in March of YR-2. As you know the patient made no complaints to me about back pain when he was presented in the emergency room on the day of the accident.

His history regarding back injury dates to February of YR-6 when he injured himself lifting a heavy box of pottery. A myleogram was administered at that time and it revealed a herniated disc at L4-L5. This injury resolved within several months through the use of heat and massage therapy, together with the use of ibuprofen. Patient reports that he has had episodes of back pain since this initial incident and before the accident in question, all of which resolved through the use of ipuprofen and short periods of rest.

Patient reports the onset of back pain within a day of the accident in question. He states that he did not seek treatment at that time because he felt, like on previous occasions, that the back pain would resolve itself. When the pain persisted and radiated down the left leg, and at times into the right thigh, patient sought the treatment of his physician, Dr. Gratch. MRI was ordered and revealed herniated discs at L4-L5 and L5-S1. Patient was treated with ibuprofen and heat and massage therapy. Back problem has abated substantially with only intermittent episodes of back pain, with some radiation down the left leg. Surgery has been ruled out as unnecessary at the present time.

I conducted a physical examination of the patient which revealed the following. Patient appears healthy and in no apparent distress. He sat for prolonged periods during the history-taking and frequently leaned forward without apparent undue discomfort. He was asked to dress with the gown and remove his socks and shoes and did this quickly. Range of motion of the major joints was normal although there was some reported discomfort elicited with straight leg raising in both legs at about 60 degrees, but with back pain alone without a radicular element. The peripheral neurologic was normal although he did manifest sensory decrease to touch and pain in the left leg in a nondermatomal distribution (the entire leg). Motor power was preserved throughout. He was able to bend forward but reported back pain at 60 degrees of hip flexion. He could walk on heals and toes without difficulty.

In summary, this is a 31-year-old man with a previous history of lumbrosacral injury that dates to his mid-twenties associated with recurrent episodes of discomfort and who now claims chronic discomfort after a motor vehicle accident. His disc disease, as demonstrated by the MRI, may be responsible for intermittent discomfort, but it is difficult to relate his chronic syptomatology to the accident of 2/11/YR-2. Lumbosacral injuries do occur in motor vehicle accidents, but these are usually of the "lap-strap" variety and occur in high-speed front-end collisions, not in accidents such as the one in which this patient was involved. Additionally, this patient had symptoms in his lumbosacral spine before the accident that required periodic treatment. His period of discomfort after the accident may have exaggerated his syptoms for a short time, but that discomfort has been substantially resolved. The more likely cause of patient's current condition is chronic degenerative disc disease, relating to his occupation as a potter, which requires many hours of sitting without break at the potter's wheel, as well as the lifting of heavy pottery which was responsible for patient's first instance of lumbosacral injury.

I thank you for the opportunity to review the records and conduct the physical examination in this matter, and should I be of any further service to you, please don't hesitate to call. My bill for service and curriculum vitae are enclosed.

Sincerely,

Rachel M. Kaplan M.D.

RACHEL M. KAPLAN, M.D.

RMK/ew
Enclosures

# RACHEL M. KAPLAN, M.D.

Greenhill Lane #809
Nita City, Nita

## EDUCATION

Pennsylvania State University - Thomas Jefferson Medical University (5 year combined medical degree program ) Degree earned - M.D. - YR-6

Nita City Memorial Hospital, Orthopaedic Residency, completed YR-2 (July)

## HONORS

Alpha Omega Alpha - YR-5

## PROFESSIONAL CERTIFICATION

Diplomat National Board of Medical Examiners - YR-4
Certified by the National Board of American College of Orthopaedic Surgery - September YR-1

## AFFILIATIONS

Drolling Hill Hospital - House Officer part time
Nita City Memorial Hospital - staff privileges

## MEMBERSHIPS

Nita County Medical Society
American Medical Association
Nita Medical Society

## APPOINTMENTS

Instructor - Senior Medical Students - University of Nita Medical School
Visiting Lecturer (University of Nita School of Nursing)

## PERSONAL

Born - Nita City, Nita - YR-29
Marital Status - Single

## ARTICLES AND LECTURES

Ellis, Kaplan, "Psychological Stresses of the Surgical Residency," 5 *Psychology Today* 22, YR-2.

McGlumphy, Kaplan, "Obstetrical Delivery and Associated Orthopaedic Nerve Blocks," *The New Physician*, YR-l.

Kaplan, "Effects of Ethanol on Bone Resorption in Patients Over 50," (unpublished), YR-l.

RACHEL M. KAPLAN, M.D.
Greenhill Lane #809
Nita City, Nita

Re: Dennis McLain

For Professional Services Rendered:

8 hours research at $125 per hour = $1,000.00

Please remit $1,000.00 at your earliest convenience.

Rachel M. Kaplan, M.D.

IN THE CIRCUIT COURT OF
DARROW COUNTY, NITA
CIVIL DIVISION

| | | |
|---|---|---|
| DENNIS McLAIN and<br>JENNIFER McLAIN,<br>Plaintiffs,<br>v.<br>ALEXANDER BARBER and<br>LYNN BARBER,<br>Defendants. | ) | CIVIL ACTION FILE<br>NO. CA-0073-R |

ORDER

The parties to this action or their attorneys having appeared before the court at a pretrial conference pursuant to Rule of Civil Procedure 16, the following action was taken:

(i) It is ordered that the following amendments to the pleadings are allowed:

(ii) The parties agreed that the trial of this action shall be based upon the pleadings as amended, except that the following issues raised by the pleadings are abandoned:

(iii) The parties stipulated to the following facts:

(iv) The parties agreed that the following documents, which were marked for identification, may be received in evidence:

(v) The parties agreed to limit the number of expert witnesses as follows:

(vi) The parties agreed that the following are all of the claims for damages or for other relief in this action, as of the date of this conference:

(vii) The parties also agreed on the following matters:

(viii) The issues to be tried are formulated by the court as follows:

The probable length of trial is ______ days. The case will be listed on the trial calendar, to be tried when reached.

IT IS ORDERED that the pretrial order may be modified at the trial of the action, or prior thereto, to prevent manifest injustice. Such modification may be made either on application of counsel for the parties or on motion of the court;

IT IS FURTHER ORDERED that requests for jury instructions shall be submitted to the trial court at the commencement of the trial, but there is reserved to counsel for the respective parties the right to submit supplemental requests for instructions during the course of the trial or at the conclusion of the evidence on matters that cannot reasonably be anticipated.

______________________________

Date:

APPROVED AS TO FORM AND SUBSTANCE

______________________________
ATTORNEY FOR PLAINTIFF(S)

______________________________
ATTORNEY FOR DEFENDANT(S)

IN THE CIRCUIT COURT OF
DARROW COUNTY, NITA
CIVIL DIVISION

| | | |
|---|---|---|
| DENNIS McLAIN and<br>JENNIFER McLAIN,<br>Plaintiffs,<br>v.<br>ALEXANDER BARBER and<br>LYNN BARBER,<br>Defendants. | ) | CIVIL ACTION FILE<br>NO. CA-0073-R |

SPECIAL INTERROGATORY VERDICT FORM
(LIABILITY ONLY)

We the Jury, after careful and thoughtful deliberations, find the following to be true:

1. Was the defendant, Alexander Barber, negligent?

_____ YES _____ NO

If the answer to Interrogatory No. 1 was "Yes," answer the following interrogatory:

2. Was the negligence of the defendant, Alexander Barber, a legal cause of the accident?

_____ YES _____ NO

3. Was the plaintiff, Dennis McLain, negligent?

_____ YES _____ NO

If your answer to Interrogatory No. 3 was "Yes," answer the following interrogatory:

4. Was the negligent conduct of the plaintiff, Dennis McLain, a legal cause of the accident?

______ YES ______ NO

If you answer Interrogatory Nos. 2 or 4 "Yes," then you <u>must</u> answer the following Interrogatory. In other words, if you determine that both Alexander Barber and Dennis McLain were negligent <u>and</u> you determine their negligence was a legal cause of the accident, then you must assign a percentage to <u>each</u> cause. If you find there was only one party who was negligent <u>and</u> a legal cause of the accident, you must assign that party as 100% at fault. If you find there was no cause of this accident, then you need not fill in the percentages.

5. Alexander Barber ______%

Dennis McLain ______%

______________________________
Jury Foreperson

IN THE CIRCUIT COURT OF
DARROW COUNTY, NITA
CIVIL DIVISION

| | | |
|---|---|---|
| DENNIS McLAIN and<br>JENNIFER McLAIN,<br>Plaintiffs,<br>v.<br>ALEXANDER BARBER and<br>LYNN BARBER,<br>Defendants. | ) | CIVIL ACTION FILE<br>NO. CA-0073-R |

SPECIAL INTERROGATORY VERDICT FORM

We the Jury, after careful and thoughtful deliberations, find the following to be true:

1. Was the defendant, Alexander Barber, negligent?

_______ YES     _______ NO

If the answer to Interrogatory No. 1 was "Yes," answer the following interrogatory:

2. Was the negligence of the defendant, Alexander Barber, a legal cause of the accident?

_______ YES     _______ NO

3. Was the plaintiff, Dennis McLain, negligent?

_______ YES     _______ NO

If your answer to Interrogatory No. 3 was "Yes," answer the following interrogatory:

4. Was the negligent conduct of the plaintiff, Dennis McLain, a legal cause of the accident?

_______ YES     _______ NO

If you answer Interrogatory Nos. 2 or 4 "Yes," then you <u>must</u> answer the following Interrogatory. In other words, if you determine that both Alexander Barber and Dennis McLain were negligent <u>and</u> you determine their negligence was a legal cause of the accident, then you must assign a percentage to <u>each</u> cause. If you find there was only one party who was negligent <u>and</u> a legal cause of the accident, you must assign that party as 100% at fault. If you find there was no cause of this accident, then you need not fill in the percentages.

5. Alexander Barber ______%

   Dennis McLain ______%

6. The plaintiff, Dennis McLain, has sustained fair and reasonable damages in the amount of $____________.

7. The plaintiff, Jennifer McLain, has sustained fair and reasonable damages in the amount of $ ___________.

____________________

JURY FOREPERSON

## JURY INSTRUCTIONS
## Closing Instruction 1

ISSUES IN THE CASE

Each plaintiff claims that he or she was injured and sustained damage as a result of the negligent conduct of the defendants. The plaintiffs have the burden of proving their claims.

OPTIONAL

The defendant, (if Lynn Barber asserts property damage claim) Lynn Barber, claims that she sustained damages as a result of the negligent conduct of the plaintiff Dennis McLain. The defendant Lynn Barber has the burden of proving her claim.

The plaintiffs and defendants deny each others' claims for personal injury or damage and have asserted certain affirmative defenses that one or all of the parties were negligent and such negligence was a substantial factor in bringing about their particular injuries. The plaintiffs and defendants, each of them, have the burden of proving the affirmative defenses.

Based upon the evidence presented at trial, the only issues for you to decide in accordance with the law as I shall give it to you are:

1. Was the defendant, Alexander Barber, negligent, and was his negligence a legal cause of the accident?

2. Was the plaintiff, Dennis McLain, negligent, and was his negligence a legal cause of the accident?

## Closing Instruction 2

NEGLIGENCE

The legal term negligence, otherwise known as carelessness, is the absence of ordinary care which a reasonable, prudent person would exercise in the circumstances here presented. Negligent conduct may consist either of an act or an omission to act when there is a duty to do so. In other words, negligence is the failure to do something which a reasonably careful person would do, or the doing of something which a reasonably careful person would not do, in light of all the surrounding circumstances established by the evidence in this case. It is for you to determine how a reasonable, careful person would act in those circumstances.

## Closing Instruction 3

ORDINARY CARE

Ordinary care is the care a reasonably careful person would use under the circumstances presented in this case. It is the duty of every person to use ordinary care not only for his own safety and protection of his property, but also to avoid injury to others. What constitutes ordinary care varies according to the particular circumstances and conditions existing then and there. The amount of care required by the law must be in keeping with the degree of danger involved.

## Closing Instruction 4

CARE OF A DRIVER

One who is operating a vehicle upon the roadway has a duty to be continuously alert, to perceive any warning of danger that is reasonably likely to exist, and to have the vehicle under such control that injury to persons or to property can be averted.

## Closing Instruction 5

The Motor Vehicle Safety Act of the State of Nita requires the drivers of motor vehicles to obey certain duties while driving. If you find that either the plaintiff or defendant violated any of the following provisions of the Act, you must find the plaintiff or defendant was negligent as a matter of law.

However, it is still up to you as the trier of fact to determine if that negligence was a substantial factor in bringing about the accident or what is called the legal cause of the accident which I will instruct you on in a few moments.

The following duties apply to all drivers of motor vehicles upon the roadways of the State of Nita:

Duty No. 1

Whenever any roadway has been divided into two or more clearly marked lanes for traffic, the following rule applies:

Driving within a single lane

(1) A vehicle shall be driven as nearly as practicable entirely within a single lane and shall not be moved from the lane until the driver has first ascertained that the movement can be made with safety.

(75 Nita N.S.A. §3309(1))

Duty No. 2

Overtaking Vehicle on the Left

(1) The driver of a vehicle overtaking another vehicle proceeding in the same direction shall pass to the left of the other vehicle at a safe distance and shall stay to the left of the vehicle until safely clear of the overtaken vehicle.

(75 Nita N.S.A. §3303 (1))

Duty No. 3

Driving Vehicle at Safe Speed

No person shall drive a vehicle at a greater speed than is reasonable and prudent under the conditions and having regard to the actual or potential hazards then existing, nor at a speed greater than will permit the driver to bring his vehicle to a stop within the assured clear distance ahead. Consistent with the foregoing, every person shall drive at a safe and appropriate speed when approaching and crossing an intersection or railroad crossing, when approaching or going around a curve, when approaching a hill crest, when traveling upon any narrow or winding roadway, and when special hazards exist with respect to pedestrians or other traffic or by reason of weather or highway conditions.

(75 Nita N.S.A. §3361)

Duty No. 4

Posted Maximum Speed

Except when a special hazard exists that requires lower speed for compliance with Duty No. 3, which I just read you, the maximum lawful speed which a person shall not drive a vehicle in excess of on U.S. Highway 76 is 50 miles per hour.

(Modification of 75 Nita N.S.A. §3362 and §3363 which establishes an alteration of maximum limits)

Duty No. 5

Driving at Reduced Speed

Except when reduced speed is necessary for safe operation or in compliance with law, no person shall drive a motor vehicle at such a slow speed as to impede the normal and reasonable movement of traffic.

(75 Nita N.S.A. §3364(a))

Duty No. 6

Posted Minimum Speed

Except when a special hazard exists that requires lower speed for compliance with Duty No. 5, which I just read you, the minimum speed limit below which no person shall drive except where necessary for safe operation on U.S. Highway 76 is 35 miles per hour.

(Modification of 75 Nita N.S.A. §3364(c) which allows posting of minimum speeds.)

Members of the Jury, you are instructed as a matter of law that for this accident the joining of the Vine Street entrance with U.S. Highway 76 East is an intersection under the laws of Nita. It is not up to you to determine if it is an intersection, but you must consider it as such. It is your job to determine if either of the parties violated the following duties which apply to driving within an intersection.

(Based upon 75 Nita N.S.A. 5102 and the cases delineated thereunder.)

**JUDGE'S NOTE: In the alternative to the instructions above as to intersections, the following duty may be read to the jury.**

Duty No. 7

Vehicle Entering or Crossing Roadway

The driver of a vehicle about to enter or cross a roadway from any place other than another roadway shall yield the right-of-way to all vehicles approaching on the roadway to be entered or crossed.

(75 Nita N.S.A. §3324)

Duty No. 8

Yield Signs

The driver of a vehicle approaching a yield sign shall in obedience to the sign slow down to a speed reasonable for existing conditions and, if required for safety to stop, shall stop before entering a crosswalk on the near side of the intersection, or, if none, then at the point nearest the intersecting roadway where the driver has a view of approaching traffic on the intersecting roadway before entering. After slowing down or stopping, the driver shall yield the right of way to any vehicle in the intersection or approaching on another roadway so closely as to constitute a hazard during the time the driver is moving across or within the intersection of roadways. If a driver is involved in a collision with a vehicle in the intersection or junction of roadways after driving past a yield sign, the collision shall be deemed prima facie evidence of failure of the driver to yield the right of way.

(75 Nita N.S.A. §3323)

**Closing Instruction 6**

LEGAL CAUSE

As I stated earlier, you must determine if either of the parties' actions were negligent, and if so, whether that negligence was a legal cause of the accident. Legal cause means: The negligent conduct must have been a substantial factor in bringing about the accident. This is what the law recognizes as legal cause. A substantial factor is an actual, real factor, although the result may be unusual or unexpected, but it is not an imaginary or fanciful factor nor a factor having no connection with the accident.

**Closing Instruction 7**

CONCURRING CAUSES

There may be more than one substantial factor in bringing about an accident. When negligent conduct of two or more persons contributes concurrently to an accident, each of these persons is fully responsible for the accident regardless of the relative extent to which each contributed to the accident. A cause is concurrent if it was operative at the moment of the accident and acted with another cause as a substantial, contributive factor in bringing about the accident.

**Closing Instruction 8**

COMPARATIVE NEGLIGENCE

If you find that one or more of the parties are negligent and that their negligence was a legal cause of the accident, it will be your responsibility to apportion the causal negligence of the parties. If you find that the plaintiff was causally negligent, this will not bar his recovery unless his causal negligence is greater than the causal negligence of the defendants against whom recovery is sought.

. . . . . . . . . . . . . .

Voir Dire questions

- experience driving in snow, what is required

- have you seen the intersection, do you know about the crazy turn of I-76

100 yds